Gender and Food

THE GENDER LENS SERIES

Series Editors

Judith A. Howard
University of Washington

Barbara Risman, editor emerita
University of Illinois, Chicago

Joey Sprague
University of Kansas

Virginia Rutter
Framingham State University

The Gender Lens series has been conceptualized as a way of encouraging the development of a sociological understanding of gender. A "gender lens" means working to make gender visible in social phenomena; asking if, how, and why social processes, standards, and opportunities differ systematically for women and men. It also means recognizing that gender inequality is inextricably braided with other systems of inequality. The Gender Lens series is committed to social change directed toward eradicating these inequalities. Originally published by Sage Publications and Pine Forge Press, all Gender Lens books are now available from The Rowman & Littlefield Publishing Group.

BOOKS IN THE SERIES

Shelley L. Koch, *Gender and Food: A Critical Look at the Food System*
Dana M. Britton, Shannon K. Jacobsen, and Grace Howard, *The Gender of Crime, Second Edition*
Joey Sprague, *Feminist Methodologies for Critical Researchers: Bridging Differences, Second Edition*
Virginia Rutter and Pepper Schwartz, *The Gender of Sexuality: Exploring Sexual Possibilities, Second Edition*
Jocelyn A. Hollander, Daniel G. Renfrow, and Judith Howard, *Gendered Situations, Gendered Selves: A Gender Lens on Social Psychology, Second Edition*
Manisha Desai, *Gender and the Politics of Possibilities*
Scott Coltrane and Michele Adams, *Gender and Families, Second Edition*
Yen Le Espiritu, *Asian American Women and Men: Labor, Laws, and Love, Second Edition*
Sara L. Crawley, Lara J. Foley, and Constance L. Shehan, *Gendering Bodies*
Oriel Sullivan, *Changing Gender Relations, Changing Families: Tracing the Pace of Change over Time*
Joan Acker, *Class Questions: Feminist Answers*
Dorothy E. Smith, *Institutional Ethnography: A Sociology for People*
Shirley A. Hill, *Black Intimacies: A Gender Perspective on Families and Relationships*
Lisa D. Brush, *Gender and Governance*
Judith Lorber and Lisa Jean Moore, *Gender and the Social Construction of Illness, Second Edition*
M. Bahati Kuumba, *Gender and Social Movements*
Toni M. Calasanti and Kathleen F. Slevin, *Gender, Social Inequities, and Aging*
Francesca M. Cancian and Stacey J. Oliker, *Caring and Gender*
Myra Marx Ferree, Judith Lorber, and Beth B. Hess, editors, *Revisioning Gender*
Michael A. Messner, *Politics of Masculinities: Men in Movements*

Gender and Food

A Critical Look at the Food System

Shelley L. Koch
Emory & Henry College

ROWMAN & LITTLEFIELD
Lanham • Boulder • New York • London

Executive Editor: Rolf Janke
Editorial Assistant: Courtney Packard
Marketing Manager: Kim Lyons

Credits and acknowledgments for material borrowed from other sources, and
reproduced with permission, appear on the appropriate page within the text.

Published by Rowman & Littlefield
A wholly owned subsidiary of The Rowman & Littlefield Publishing Group, Inc.
4501 Forbes Boulevard, Suite 200, Lanham, Maryland 20706
www.rowman.com

6 Tinworth Street, London SE11 5AL, United Kingdom

British Library Cataloguing in Publication Information Available

Library of Congress Cataloging-in-Publication Data Available

ISBN 9781442257757 (cloth : alk. paper)
ISBN 9781442257733 (pbk. : alk. paper)
ISBN 9781442257740 (electronic)

♾™ The paper used in this publication meets the minimum requirements of
American National Standard for Information Sciences—Permanence of Paper for
Printed Library Materials, ANSI/NISO Z39.48-1992.

Printed in the United States of America

Contents

Acknowledgments

This project began with a fortuitous conversation with Joey Sprague. She was interviewing me for a project she was working on, and when we were chatting after the interview, I asked her if she could direct me to any current scholarship on gender inequality across the food system. In true Joey fashion, she said she didn't know of anything but asked, "Why don't you write about it?" I've spent the last four years researching a project I am passionate about: understanding how systems of inequality, especially gender, structure the food system. Without Joey's encouragement and mentorship, I don't think this project would have come to fruition. I can't thank her enough for the many years of support she's provided, even in her retirement! The team at Rowman & Littlefield also helped make this project possible, especially Sarah Stanton, who patiently nudged me along, and Rolf Janke and Courtney Packard, who pushed the project over the finish line.

I have been fortunate to receive considerable institutional support for this project. Emory & Henry College provided a research grant and pretenure leave. This leave would not have been possible without the backing of Ed Davis. The Appalachian Colleges Association granted me a postdoctoral faculty fellowship to complete the research for the project. Without assistance from the librarians at Emory & Henry—Patty Greany, Jody Hanshew, and Jane Caldwell, in particular—I would not have been able to access the necessary resources. I also want to thank my good friends Kelly Bremner, Alma Ramirez, Travis Proffitt, and Mark Finney for their camaraderie over the course of this project.

Many people contributed feedback on drafts. I received excellent comments from colleagues at Association for the Study of Food and Society conferences as well as students in a new course on food and inequality. They offered critical feedback from the undergraduate perspective, and I thank them for allowing me to test these chapters on them. Steve Fisher also provided thorough and insightful comments in his review of several chapters. I thank him for that and his continued friendship.

Of course, I have to thank my family for their effort in this process. I spent most of three years writing during holidays and in the summers, and they not only did not complain but read countless drafts and revisions. Meredith in particular helped with my edits even as she was writing her own thesis, Gary read chapters multiple times, and Haydyn was always cheering me on when I got frustrated. Much love and many thanks to them. My father, Dick Koch, hosted me for several weeks and plied me with coffee to keep me writing. My mother, LaVernne Koch, passed away during the course of this project. Even though she favored novels over academic manuscripts, she enthusiastically supported my work and would have been delighted to show off this book to her friends. I dedicate this book to her.

CHAPTER 1

Introduction

> Understanding why, where, and how oppression manifests itself within the food system, recognizing it within our food movement and organizations (and within ourselves), is not extra work for transforming the food system. It *is* the work.
>
> (Holt-Gimenez 2017, 232)

Although I didn't grow up on a farm, living in the cornhusker state of Nebraska I was surrounded by agriculture. My first paid job was roguing corn. The farmer gave a group of young teenagers very sharp knives and hauled us out to a field at six o'clock in the morning to cut out "rogue" corn, plants growing outside the row. We'd walk the fields until early afternoon, when it got too hot, and then go to the swimming pool for the rest of the day. Fast-forward many years, and I found myself shopping and cooking for two young daughters as a graduate student in sociology. The pressure to feed my kids "healthy" food was intense and provided the impetus for me to study how grocery shoppers make sense of their work as the subject of my dissertation.

I recognize my experience with the food system has been shaped by my social location as a white, middle-class, highly educated woman. My farmwork experience was a summer job to make extra money to spend on teenage consumption; for many farmworkers, their work is critical to their family's survival. Even though I was on a graduate student stipend while earning my PhD, my spouse's income allowed me to buy food without worrying about going hungry. My perspective is also shaped by my being a citizen of the United States and thus the Global North, a position that privileges me in access to food, education, information, and wealth. I acknowledge that I'm writing this book from this vantage.

But climate change now draws the world—developed and developing countries and the people who live in them—together in unexpected ways. My kids and their generation will have to survive in a world that is hotter, more unpredictable, and more conflictual each year as sea levels rise and drought, famine, and food scarcity displace people and push them into others' homelands. As citizens of the Global North, educated, and white, they will probably have the best chance of survival. But for the millions of poor people living on the world's coasts, or the mothers who will have to find food for their children, or the nonhuman creatures fighting for survival, their chances diminish the longer we wait to address fundamental problems in our social systems that have led us to this moment. The industrial agricultural system, which includes growing, distributing, preparing, and eating food, plays a major role in our global environmental problems. Before I examine the contemporary industrial agricultural system—agrifood for short—I'd like to provide a historical contrast to highlight the truly exceptional character of the modern food system.

CAN FOOD SYSTEMS BE SUSTAINABLE?

For about 90 percent of human history, our ancestors used hunting and gathering to procure their food. Almost everyone in these small societies participated in the production and consumption of food, either by hunting animals or gathering nuts, berries, and other foodstuffs. Food was eaten immediately, making this food system the least complex. While people might consider this type of society "primitive," hunters and gatherers were able to feed and reproduce themselves and their society sustainably for thousands of years. Although a gendered division of labor existed whereby men hunted and women foraged and cooked, academics believe these societies were also much less stratified, or unequal, than industrial societies today (Smith 1997).

People began purposefully growing food—small-scale horticulture and agriculture—around ten thousand years ago. Most small-scale agriculture was still very local.[1] I want to describe one example of a traditional small-scale agricultural system, as it will provide a stark contrast to our current food system. Gilbert Wilson's graduate dissertation, published in 1917 as *Buffalo Bird Woman's Garden*, is a collection of eyewitness accounts and interviews with women agriculturalists of the upper Plains Native American tribes, the Mandan, Hidatsa, and Arikara, located in what is today North Dakota, Montana, and Wyoming (Wilson [1917] 1987). The tribes' growing and processing system was based on the interconnected planting and harvesting of corn, squash, and beans, also known as "the three sisters." In this growing system, corn stalks provided a trellis for the beans, the beans added nitrogen to the soil, and the squash spread out along the ground to prevent weeds from growing under the other plants. These foods were also nutritionally complementary and included what we now call proteins and carbohydrates. Although the hunting of local game supplemented the three sisters, they alone met a majority of the dietary needs of these tribes. While scholars don't have specific data on what proportion of the total food intake these crops accounted for in these Great Plains tribes, women's food production provided an estimated 65 to 85 percent of the total caloric intake of hunting-and-gathering societies as well as traditional indigenous Native American societies (R. Lee 1979; Merchant 1989).

Women, as the main agriculturalists in these Native tribes, drew on an integrated system of experiential and traditional knowledges to guide them in planting, harvesting, and eating food. They planted corn when the gooseberry bush began to leaf, though not before engaging in a sacred ritual dance to ask the gods for a good growing season. This type of agriculture was very labor-intensive. Here is Buffalo Bird Woman recounting how corn was planted:

> Around each of the old and dead hills I loosened the soil with my hoe, first pulling up the old, dead roots of the previous year's plants; these dead roots, as they collected, were raked off with other refuse to one end of the field outside of the cultivated ground, to be burned. This pulling up of the dead roots and working around the old hill with the hoe, left the soil soft and loose for the space of about eighteen inches in diameter; and in this soft soil I planted the corn in this manner: I stooped over, and with fingers of both hands I raked away the loose soil for a bed for the seed; and with my fingers I even stirred the soil around with a circular motion to make the bed perfectly level so that the seeds would all lie at the same depth. A small vessel, usually a wooden bowl, at my feet held the seed corn. With my right hand I took a small handful of the corn, quickly transferring half of it to my left hand; still stooping over, and plying both hands at the same time, I pressed the grains a half inch into the soil with my thumbs, planting two grains at a time, one with each hand. I planted about six to eight grains in a hill. Then with my hands I raked the earth over the planted grains until the seed lay about the length of my fingers under the soil. Finally I patted the hill firm with my palms. (Wilson 1917 [1987], 22)

After planting, weeding, and hoeing throughout the summer, the older women would determine when the time was right for green corn harvesting by looking at the plant's outer appearance: they would know green corn was ready for plucking by the dry brown tassels, the dry silks, and the dark green husks; they never had to open the ear to see if it was in good green corn condition (Peters 1995, 117). At the main harvest, the timing of which was again determined by the women, it was their sacred duty to ensure that every ear of corn was gathered and used for some purpose, whether it was cooked, or the kernels were dried and ground for bread, or the seed was saved for the next growing season. The same women also prepared the food for everyday consumption and preserved it for storage for traveling and for the long winter months.

The food system of these tribes enabled them to provide basic sustenance to their members while remaining in ecological balance. In contrast, our contemporary industrial agrifood system, centered on and controlled by farmers, governments, and businesses in the Global North and especially the United States, is a system in ecological crisis. Corn is also a staple of our agrifood system, but the difference between how the Native tribes grew and used corn and how we do is stark. In 2015 U.S. farmers grew 13.6 billion bushels of corn on 90 million acres of land (USDA 2016a). Farmers can grow so much because they rely on a monoculture system in which only one type of food is grown in massive quantities. Instead of planting and harvesting by hand, farmers use machines such as tractors, combines, and harvesters that can cost up to $500,000 and are powered by fossil fuels. Instead of using intercropping such as the three sisters to nourish the soil and provide insect protection, farmers use synthetic fertilizers made in factories using natural gas and apply toxic pesticides to remove insects and keep diseases from the plants.

Although this system produces an enormous amount of food, it destroys soil and water resources in the process. Farmers add so much fertilizer that the ground cannot absorb it all, and these chemicals end up in our waterways, fertilizing the growth of algae, which zaps oxygen out of the water. This process has created "dead zones," areas in which no fish or sea life can survive. Corn also needs a lot of water, up to three thousand gallons for each bushel of yield, which has depleted underground water tables. In addition, agricultural practices worldwide account for 24 percent of greenhouse gas emissions, including 52 percent of global methane and 84 percent of global nitrous oxide emissions (Intergovernmental Panel on Climate Change 2014). For all this activity, we eat less than 20 percent of the corn we grow; about 40 percent is used to make ethanol to power our cars and other machines, while 36 percent goes to feed cattle (USDA 2018; Foley 2013).

Although it may look like farmers don't care about the land, in reality they are responding to the policies and demands of the globalized agricultural system. Many small farmers have trouble making ends meet because prices for their crops are so low, and young people are often reluctant to go into farming because of the difficulty of making a living. Paradoxically, the U.S. corn trade is decimating small corn farmers in other countries such as Mexico because they cannot compete with U.S. farmers, who receive money from the federal government (called subsidies) to plant so much corn.

In order to make money off all this excess corn, businesses invent new products such as high-fructose corn syrup (HFCS), which is used to sweeten everything from soda to yogurt to bread. Between 1970 and 1990 there was a 1,000 percent increase in the consumption of HFCS, and the average American consumed about 35.7 pounds of it in 2004 (Bray, Nielson, and Popkin 2004). Paradoxically, the American government advises consumers to eat foods that are low in added sugars such as (you guessed it!) HFCS, as these empty calories have contributed to health problems like obesity and diabetes. Sadly, 42 million Americans are still hungry, and 811 million people, the vast majority of whom live in developing countries in the world, do not have enough food to lead healthy, active lives (Food and Agriculture Organization 2017).

This system is unsustainable, and many scholars, activists, and organizations are working on ways to make it more sustainable and just (Patel 2012; Gottlieb and Joshi 2010; Alkon and Agyeman 2011; Guthman 2011; Holt-Gimenez 2017). However, one crucial piece often missing in these analyses is the role gender inequality plays in determining who gets to eat what, who grows our food, and even who picks it. In essence, gender affects all aspects of the food system. While feminists and gender scholars from all over the world are producing excellent research on gender and food, there is a lack of scholarship bringing this research together in a systemic way to highlight the significance of gender in the food system as a whole.[2] The aim of this book, then, is to synthesize previous scholarship using a gender lens to systematically illuminate the ways that gender structures the food system. Although much of the analysis is from a Western perspective, particularly an American one, I do attempt to bring in scholarship from developing countries to highlight the ways in which the agrifood system impacts the food systems of these areas as well.

Why is a gendered analysis of the food system necessary? First, it exposes structural inequalities, which presents new vantage points from which to develop research agendas as well as propel activism. For example, a gendered perspective on the food system allows us to analyze domestic cooking and cooking for wages as part of the same system: women's unpaid foodwork is expected but devalued in the home, and the capitalist agrifood system is predicated on paying women (and devalued men) less for food service and farmwork. We cannot understand one disadvantage without acknowledging the other, which makes a holistic vision of the food system imperative. A gendered analysis also offers insight into the crisis between industrial agriculture and the environment, as well as the negative human health outcomes the industrial system produces. A masculine approach to controlling and dominating the natural world undergirds industrial agriculture as well as the exploitation of women and people of color. At the microlevel, individual feminine and masculine identities are created and sustained in relationship to food. Focusing only on gender, though, is not enough to truly get at the heart of the system; we must factor in race, class, ethnicity, nationality, sexuality, religion, and a range of other social positions in order to understand how this system advantages some over others. The next section sets up the conceptual framework for synthesizing the scholarship I present in the upcoming chapters.

GENDERED INSTITUTIONS, LABOR, AND IDENTITIES

In all societies, people must coordinate their activities in order to survive. In contemporary Western industrial societies, capitalist ideas and practices coordinate the food system. One distinguishing feature of this system is the conceptual separation between the public sphere of the market and the private sphere of the home. The public sphere is where production takes place. It is the arena in which we make things like cars and phones, where we go to our jobs that provide us a paycheck, where some of us make decisions about taxes and land use. The private sphere is where the everyday tasks of living occur. We sleep and eat, raise our families, and entertain friends in our homes. This separation doesn't really exist at the level of practice, of course, as the same activity can take place in both spheres (Sprague 1988). For example, we eat at home around the dinner table, but we also eat in restaurants where we pay people to cook for us. We care for children in the home, but we also enroll our children in day care.

Gender is fundamental to this separation: the public sphere of paid labor is coded masculine, and the private sphere of the household is coded feminine (Acker 2006; Nelson 1993; Smith 2005). The public sphere of politics, economics, and business—and those who do this labor—is valued more than the private sphere of social reproduction and caregiving (Acker 2006). Not only does this dichotomy create a hierarchy of labor, but the spheres are thought to be mutually exclusive. The (public) market is dominated by an operating logic of efficiency, rationality, competition, and accumulation (Connell 2005; Connell and Messerschmidt 2005) and coordinated by relations of ruling, which are the organizations and practices that coordinate and control production, finance, distribution, and other noneconomic processes such as education and other state functions (Smith 1987, 2005). The public is the realm in which business takes place, not the realm in which caring or provisioning occurs. The private home, a place of nurturing and caring for others, is where these tasks occur. In other words, nurturing and caring for human beings, which includes feeding others, is not only subordinate to economic activities but is also missing from the goals of the capitalist market (Acker 2006, 88). Reproductive and caring labor is consequently devalued in both realms.

Within the formal economy (the public sphere), the work that women do is valued less than men's, often because men and women work in different jobs. Occupations, such as doctor and firefighter, that include skills associated with men, such as machines or authority, are often stereotyped as men's work and have higher concentrations of men. Occupations like teacher or nurse, which include caring and emotional labor, are stereotyped as women's jobs and consequently have more women working in them. Men's jobs are afforded higher status and pay than women's jobs, due in large measure to the unequal gender balance in the occupation as well as the devaluation of the work done by women (Levanon, England, and Allison 2009).

In an example from the food system, segregation exists between occupations oriented to agriculture and those oriented to nutrition. Agricultural scientists who research ways to increase the efficiency of agricultural products are mostly men. Dieticians who advise people on what to eat in order to lead a healthy lifestyle are mostly women. The median annual wage for agricultural and food scientists in 2016 was $62,920 (U.S. Bureau of Labor Statistics [BLS] 2017b), while the average dietician makes $58,920 (BLS 2017c). Even in the same occupation, men's work is more highly valued than women's work. Men are more likely to be executive chefs who manage entire kitchens, for example, while more women are pastry chefs (Harris and Guiffre 2015). While this is an overly simplified discussion of a very complex issue, it points to the fact that this gendered division of labor is fundamental to understanding how gender creates inequality regimes in our food system (Acker 2006).

Gender, of course, is not the only source of inequality in the food system. Race, class, age, sexuality, and nationality also affect who does what work and how this work is valued. Intersectionality provides the lens to explore the ways that gender and race, class, age, nationality, and ethnicity are mutually constructing systems of power (Hill Collins 2000). In other words, systems of inequality do not operate individually but rather intersect in ways that further disadvantage some people over others. Deborah Barndt (2008) untangles the story of the global tomato, a tale in which people and food cross borders through a gendered, raced, and classed food system. While global organizations structure the agrifood process, individuals in the same hemisphere can be both advantaged and disadvantaged in the same system. The female Canadian clerk who scans a tomato for a customer in Loblaws (a Canadian grocery store), for example, has more rights as a Canadian citizen than the Mexican woman farmworker who works in Canada picking tomatoes, but she is paid much less than men in upper management in the supermarket. Both the female farmworker and the clerk, however, are still responsible for feeding the individuals in their households and are accountable for the cultural expectations of health for themselves and those who depend on them.

If the public sphere is a masculine domain, the private household is constructed as women's (and thus a feminine) sphere. Women are responsible for the domestic and emotional labor involved in maintaining households and reproducing people, unpaid but necessary social labor. In terms of foodwork like cooking, shopping, and cleaning, women cook and clean four times as often as men globally (Miranda 2011, 25), while in the United States and Canada women do at least twice as much foodwork as men (BLS 2015a; Australian Bureau of Statistics 2009; Statistics Canada 2015). While men today are doing more housework than their fathers, they are still not doing as much on average as women. In general, work performed in the home to care for others is valued less in terms of remuneration and status than outside-of-home work performed for a wage (England 2010; England and Folbre 1999).

The critical point here is that while conceptually these spheres are mutually exclusive, in real life each has an impact on the other (Glucksman 1995; England and Farkas 1986). (White) men are in positions of power in the public sphere and are not expected to do emotional or caring labor in either sphere. Women are expected to do caring work such as feeding in both spheres but are disadvantaged by a lack of power in the public sphere and the expectations for reproduction in the private sphere. Thus, women who care for others in the home, particularly mothers, are disadvantaged over fathers and women without children. Scholars have shown that mothers but not fathers experience employment discrimination (Correll, Benard, and Paik 2007); employed mothers suffer a per-child wage penalty of approximately 5 percent on average (Budig and England 2001); and the pay gap between mothers and nonmothers for women under the age of thirty-five is larger than the pay gap between men and women (Crittenden 2001).

In addition to creating this (false) dichotomy of private/public, we also separate humans from nature, which leads to an orientation of domination over rather than coexistence with nature. Carolyn Merchant (1980) describes how the rise of a masculine scientific worldview ushered in a change in how we understood our relationship with the natural world, leading to the treatment of nature as a "thing" rather than a living being. Prior to the Industrial Revolution, Western society equated nature with the feminine and venerated or at least respected nature, since "she" had the power to give and take life. With the advent of the scientific revolution, nature became something that scientists could predict through experiments, control through new technologies, and reduce conceptually to inert matter. Rather than a powerful entity that possessed a living spirit, nature became a subject for scientific study and control. These mechanistic views of the world allowed the scientist (and farmer and industrialist) to control and dominate nature, since nature was now rendered predictable, regular, and subject to rules and laws.

This change in worldview, coupled with a new economic system, allowed scientists and industrialists to produce new forms of technology, which radically altered the practice of growing food. During the Industrial Revolution of the eighteenth and nineteenth centuries, human and animal labor was increasingly replaced by machines, such as the cotton gin that separated lint from seed, the mechanical thrasher that separated seed from stalk, the John Deere tractor that plowed more cleanly, and the McCormick reaper, which cut the grain. These technologies ushered in the most recent "revolution" in agriculture, known as the "mechanical revolution" (Carolan 2012). Machinery and subsequent technologies took the place of human labor and natural processes and enabled the production of significant amounts of surplus food with fewer bodies.

Industrial agricultural science, then, is based on a reductionist knowledge system that simplifies processes to parts. Mainstream agricultural scientists are less concerned with a holistic or ecological understanding of the agricultural system than with increasing yields or inventing a standardized variety. This scientific knowledge is acknowledged as the only valid or legitimate form of agricultural knowledge, and other forms of knowing are ignored, denigrated, or even appropriated. An egregious example, ultimately unsuccessful, was the case of a U.S. company that attempted to patent a derivative solution of the neem tree in India, which Indians had used for thousands of years as an organic pesticide. As Vandana Shiva (1993) argues, "Experts and specialists are thus projected as the only legitimate seekers after and producers of knowledge" (25). Thus, our industrial food system prioritizes a technical (masculine) logic based on domination, efficiency, and profit, while women's experiential knowledge with food, as well as indigenous or cultural knowledges, are often ignored or belittled as backward or primitive.

This reductionist approach to food extends to nutrition knowledge. Under a Western scientific framework, scientists, doctors, and educators reduce food to parts—vitamins, calories, and carbohydrates, for example—and create a standardized, rationalized system. G. Scrinis (2013) terms this ideology "nutritionalism," which he argues has been the dominant paradigm for nutrition science for the past century and has also become the foundation of dietary guidelines since the 1960s and food marketing since the 1980s. Nutrition science reduces food to nutrients to allow experts to make recommendations for what to eat based on these scientific parts regardless of the holistic health of the foods, traditional knowledges about food, and individual tastes. Together, these two processes—a reductionist science coupled with capitalist patterns of accumulation—shift our ideas of food as a life-sustaining necessity to food as a commodity, a product to sell on the market in exchange for money (Patel 2012; Holt-Gimenez 2017). Nutrition is also reduced from a system of ideas about how to best nourish bodies to criteria based on quantification and calculation (Mudry et al. 2014).

MASCULINITIES AND FEMININITIES

These dichotomies—home/market, private/public, humans/nature—are sustained and justified through cultural ideas about masculinity and femininity and expectations for masculine or feminine bodies. These expectations are not immutable, nor are they a consequence of biology—each society has its own scripts for what it considers appropriate for each sex, and even within societies there may be several forms of each, masculini*ties* and feminini*ties*, depending on the particular social context (Connell and Messerschmidt 2005). While masculinity and femininity are never static and always depend on the particular society and historical period for content, these qualities are not just aspects of individual identities or displays of individuals; they are also integral to how our organizations, institutions, and societies operate. As Mimi Schippers (2007) writes, "Social practice, in all its forms, from embodied interaction to child raising, sexual activity, developing and executing policy, passing legislation, producing television programming, and invading countries, is the mechanism by which masculinities and femininities, as part of a vast network of gender meanings, comes to organize social life" (92).

Characteristics of a contemporary Western masculinity include domination, competition, strength, technical control, and breadwinning, while femininity, then, is the opposite: nurturing, subordinate, cooperative, caring. For our discussion of the food system, variations of masculinity include a business masculinity, associated with the urban middle class and global financial management, which relies heavily on a technical rationality and expertise as legitimation of leadership (Connell 1995). Another variation is an agrarian masculinity that involves characteristics of endurance, physical strength, independence, control over nature, and providing for the family. These can be competing masculinities, but as they are often associated with white males, they are afforded a higher status over alternate or subordinate forms of masculinity. At all times, however, femininities are subordinate to masculinities (Connell 1995; Connell and Messerschmidt 2005).

Male dominance and power over women as a characteristic of masculinity supports the continued acts of violence against women in both the public sphere of employment as sexual harassment and in the private sphere of the home as domestic violence. The intersection of masculine dominance and Western ideas about human uniqueness also sustains the dominance over nature and natural resources. Capitalism as a system, then, is based on violence and masculine power over women, natural resources, and colonized people (Merchant 1980; Mies 1993). Maria Mies (1993, 46) argues that capitalism, as an accumulation process, was made possible not only by turning the relationship between humans and nature into one of domination but also by turning colonized people in the Global South into primitive "others" and appropriating their land and resources.

Thus, ecofeminists argue that the oppression of women, indigenous peoples, and the environment is inextricably linked because a capitalist patriarchy subordinates and exploits both carework and nature. A feminist standpoint (Harding 1986; Smith 2005) is helpful in reminding us that women are not connected to nature by any biological necessity. Rather, carework is a feminized activity relegated to the private sphere and denigrated in the public sphere. Caring for others is an integral part of femininity, to which women are then held accountable (Sachs et al. 2016, 22). In industrial societies, although women have seen significantly increased participation in the labor force, they are still responsible for foodwork and health in ways that make them more attuned to and responsible for human health and the environment.

Women are not only closer to caring processes but also disproportionately disadvantaged by the effects of environmental destruction. Deforestation, desertification, water and land pollution, blocked access to clean water and fertile land, toxins, the harmful effects of hazardous wastes, even climate change—all consequences of a capitalist economic system—directly affect women's lives and ability to provision. In areas where women cook without electricity, they are responsible for gathering energy sources and water. Effects of climate change such as desertification or causes such as deforestation mean women must travel farther to gather wood for fires and get water for cooking, which in turn takes time away from caregiving and/or agriculture. Girls who help their mothers with this work may not have time for education if these resources become too scarce. Women in general suffer when food is scarce, as they are more likely to forgo food in favor of men and children. Women in the Global North who are affected by environmental toxins like pesticides or lead in drinking water spend more time and resources taking care of their households, and even women with resources spend more time cooking and shopping to avoid these same toxins in their food so they don't get into their children's bodies (Mackendrick 2014). From the perspective of women, then, food and environmental issues are issues of survival (Shiva 1993).

PRIVILEGING THE MARKET: NEOLIBERALISM

The impact of a gendered industrial food system on women, children, people of color, the poor, and the environment is compounded by a particularly virulent economic ideology that has permeated much of the current global economy. Neoliberalism, a political economic theory that sprung out of global economic troubles of the 1970s, has drastically affected the policy and practice of national and international institutions. Neoliberalism charges that human well-being is best enhanced through strong individual property rights, free markets, and free trade, and the most effective way to help society is to give free rein to the human entrepreneurial spirit. Supporting entrepreneurs, this philosophy states, will spur innovation and competition, further improving economic competition, quality, and success. To achieve free markets, neoliberals believe that governments should step out of the way by privatizing public resources, reducing public spending on social services, eliminating regulations on businesses, reducing taxes, and limiting the labor movement's power over business (Harvey 2005). Often, however, it is women who shoulder many of the negative consequences of neoliberal economic development. Women as caregivers adjust to the decrease in public support by increasing their own economic activity, suppressing their own needs, or both.

Rolling back or eliminating state regulation is one of the primary goals of neoliberals, allegedly because state regulation is a drag on the economy. In theory, corporations will step up and police themselves through voluntary agreements and market-based measures. For example, while marketing junk food to children is illegal in many countries, the U.S. government in 2011 issued voluntary principles for corporate self-regulation, which corporations balked at as too restrictive. Many of the large manufacturers agreed to self-regulate under the Children's Food and Beverage Advertising Initiative; however, actual reductions in marketing of unhealthy foods to youth have been quite limited. This lack of public regulation means that household food provisioners are now responsible for the negative consequences of children "nagging" for the fast food they just saw on their screens or on a billboard near their school.

Defunding or underfunding government agencies and programs is another way to minimize the effects of regulation for corporations and market actors. However, this can directly endanger food consumers. In 2009, a salmonella outbreak in peanut factories in Georgia killed eight people and sickened an estimated nineteen thousand others. At the time Georgia had only sixty inspectors to monitor sixteen thousand food businesses, some of which were not inspected for a decade (Moss 2009). The defunding of social services such as the Supplemental Nutrition Assistance Program (SNAP) and nutrition programs in public schools hits households particularly hard, as many low-income individuals and parents rely on these services to provide food for their households. Food pantries and food banks, often run by nongovernmental or church organizations, have stepped into the void and are the dominant means by which the United States addresses hunger (Fisher 2017).

Even the alternative food movement offers market-based solutions to the problems created by industrial agriculture, such as expanding markets for local and organic food through farmers' markets, urban food cooperatives, and health food stores (Alkon 2014; Alkon and Guthman 2017). These solutions do not fix the problems where they first occur, such as by regulating pesticides before they are sprayed on fields or addressing inequalities in residential development that lead to neighborhoods without grocery stores. Instead, these solutions require producers and consumers, rather than political or economic leaders, to make adjustments. Alison Hope Alkon (2014) argues, "While this is certainly empowering, the lack of a role for government policy and its replacement with nongovernmental organizations and markets helps relieve the state of its responsibility to provide environmental protection and a social safety net" (30).

In addition to minimized government regulation and funding, neoliberal discourse also emphasizes the responsibility of the individual for solving social problems. In terms of nutrition, for example, a responsible citizen educates herself about the latest nutrition advice and puts it into practice through the right kind of consumption or market behavior in order to be "healthy." But in a neoliberal environment, individual responsibility for health acquires moral overtones, and achieving health becomes one's moral duty (Crawford 1980). This leads to blaming individuals who fail to live up to expectations (which often happens if one is "overweight") rather than making changes in the public sphere to solve the problem.

In general, the food system in the Global North is expert driven and based on an industrial technology. This system is structured by overlapping dichotomies—market/household, public/private, humans/nature—which are legitimated by cultural expectations for masculinity and femininity. The chapters in this book will use this framework to explore how gender is central to the practices of our food system, including growing, shopping, cooking, and eating.

STRUCTURE OF THE BOOK

In order to tease out how the food system is systemically structured by gender, this book is divided into chapters based on some of the main processes in the food system: production (growing), distribution (shopping), preparation (cooking), and eating (Sobal, Kahn, and Bisogni 1998). These categories are conceptual abstractions, of course; in practice there is much overlap between activities such as cooking and eating or cooking and grocery shopping. This ordering of different levels or subsystems, however, provides a means to explore the public and private aspects of each system in tandem, processes that, due to the supposed separation between the home and the market, are often researched and written about separately but are intimately connected and in fact often depend on the hierarchy of the public over the private.

The production system entails the growing and processing of our food. Most of us probably think of the farmer as the main player in this system. In the United States, farmers make up less than 2 percent of the population, but of those, more than 70 percent are men. In much of the developing world, at least half the population farms, and many of these farmers are women. In each case, however, who gets to claim the title of farmer is a political and gendered process. Many people grow food, but only those who grow for the market are considered farmers, a designation that allows access to government aid for credit, insurance, and other subsidies necessary to keep farms afloat in a global capitalist economy. Many people—often women, people of color, or the poor—grow food for the household or community, but we call them gardeners, not farmers, and they do their work without supports and subsidies. This divide is significant as it affects people's access to food.

The jobs in production and processing are ordered by gender as well as race, ethnicity, and nationality. Not only are more men farmers in the developed world, but women also have a more difficult time breaking into farming due to the masculine farmer stereotype, which can lead to a lack of training to prepare women for farming, as well as discrimination by agricultural and financial agents in accessing credit and aid. In addition, large multinational companies that provide the seeds and other inputs have a considerable amount of power in this system, while the workers who pick our food are nearly invisible. I treat these issues in more depth in chapter 2.

The distribution system organizes how the food moves from the farm into the consumer's hands and includes transporting, storing, processing, packaging, wholesaling, and retailing. While this system generates about 28 percent of the profit in the food system, it is the least studied from a gender and food perspective. In chapter 3 I explore one aspect of the distribution system—food retail—and find a pronounced gendered division of labor, with women working in service positions in grocery stores, while (white) men occupy management and executive positions. A gendered division of household labor also exists at the level of grocery shopping. Women are still the primary grocery shoppers, and a food femininity shapes the expectation that good mothers and spouses will buy their families healthy food. Managers and owners of supermarkets and grocery stores, often men, organize the store to get shoppers to spend as much money as possible rather than to help shoppers buy good food for their families. Alternative shopping venues like farmers' markets often add to the work of shopping. Race and class also shape access to food and one's ability to provision the household.

Cooking or preparing food is the aspect of the food system that has the most developed gender scholarship. Feminist scholars have examined the household division of food and how a feminine or masculine identity both shapes and is shaped by food and foodwork. In the United States we spend about the same amount of money on eating out as we do on cooking for ourselves, so often other people are making our meals. In general, people of color are cooking in these kitchens, and women are serving us. In high-end restaurants, however, men do much of the cooking and serving *and* receive better wages and status. However, workers' health can suffer in these masculine environments with a focus on competition and pushing limits. I discuss these processes in more detail in chapter 4.

Gender shapes what and how we eat. In chapter 5 I explore how feminine food and eating is light and minimal, while masculine food and eating is hearty and filling. Expectations for certain body types have different consequences for men and women. Even what we know about nutrition is a product of a gendered epistemology (system of knowing). In this system, abstract (masculine) rationality privileges counting and abstraction over experiential or applied knowledge. In terms of the mainstream conception of food and nutrition, Western (and particularly American) nutrition is quantified, standardized, reduced to nutrients, and divorced from the social context in which we eat, often leading to a dysfunctional relationship to food.

In the conclusion I bring these issues together and find common themes that run throughout the food system. If our industrial agricultural system is bound to a masculine economic system based on domination, technology, competition, and profit over survival, then to change this system we must change how we define and value masculinity and femininity, how we reward and value jobs and caring, and the gendered power structure itself. This requires a gender lens.

NOTES

1. This is a gross oversimplification. Civilizations such as the Roman Empire, Chinese dynasties, and Mesoamerican empires were based on exploiting the work of peasants or the enslaved.

2. Although many researchers are working on gender and the food system, these articles are particularly relevant for a feminist overview of the food system: Allen and Sachs 2007; Avakian and Haber 2005.

CHAPTER 2

Growing

Living in Kansas, I would frequently pass a sign on the side of the highway sponsored by Kansas Agri-Women that read, "A Kansas farmer feeds 128 people, and you!" I don't remember if the sign included a picture of a farmer, but if it did, I imagine it would be a white, middle-aged man in overalls driving a tractor—the stereotypical image of the person who grows food in Western society. Statistically, this image is not far from reality, at least in the United States: the average American farmer is a fifty-eight-year-old white man. The industrial food system relies on these farmers to produce large quantities of food (as the sign suggests) in the form of commodities (food to be traded on the market) to be transformed into the products on our grocery store shelves.

This stereotypical image is deceptive in several ways. First, not all farmers are men. Many women farm in both the Global North and South, but this work is not necessarily captured in agricultural statistics. Second, a single farmer does not complete all the work necessary to run a farm. Farmworkers who are not related to the farmer pick, sort, and transport crops. Spouses also work on the farm, and if they are women, they do many farm-related chores, run the household, and care for the children, not to mention bringing in much-needed off-farm income. The stereotypical farmer image also suggests that only "official" farmers grow food to feed us. This is not true. Many people, especially in developing countries, grow food for their households or communities but do not necessarily sell this food to others or feed 127 additional people. This image also assumes that farmers get to choose what kind of food gets grown. This is also not the case. Multinational corporations and government policies greatly constrain the kind of food the farmer can grow.

Inequalities, especially those rooted in gender, race, class, and nationality, structure each facet of food production I've introduced above. Whether the farmer is growing food for sale on the market or for subsistence certainly plays an important role in reproducing inequality, as work that is done for the market is valued and listed in statistics to be counted, while work done for the farm household is taken for granted and therefore rendered invisible. Within each occupation (farmer, farmworker, corporate manager), there is a hierarchical gendered division of labor supported by notions of what is appropriate for men and women (masculinity and femininity). These jobs are also organized by skin color or citizenship status. In this chapter I look at who is growing our food, how these jobs are valued, and the gendered (and raced) distribution of power at the corporate, scientific, and government levels. Let's start with how Western society classifies farmers and farms.

WHO IS MY FARMER?

While a gendered division of labor in agriculture has existed in every society, who actually does the work of growing food depends on the type of agriculture of that society and the general level of private ownership of property. The Plains tribal example in chapter 1 would be considered a female farming system, whereby women are in charge of the knowledge and labor involved in growing, planting, harvesting, and storing, and men do little agricultural work (Boserup 1970). Prior to European settlement, many Native American societies depended on women's agriculture, and women had access to land and resources through matrilineal descent (Sachs 1996).[1]

Men's farming systems tended to take over when permanent fields were established. These systems often involved draft animals and, later, mechanical devices such as the tractor, as well as a more pronounced private ownership of land and property. In other words, the transition from female labor to male labor became more apparent as capitalism developed (Boserup 1970; Sachs 1996; Holt-Gimenez 2017). The U.S. agricultural system, which provides the basis of the global industrial agricultural system, follows a male-dominated farming system in which mechanization and patrilineal ownership is central (Merchant 1989). In these systems, men tend to take responsibility for the fields while women are in charge of the household, and land is passed down from fathers to sons. In the U.S. system, farming is also a white institution, as whites enslaved African Americans to labor on plantations or kept them from owning land under the tenancy system.

A male farming system does not mean that women do not do work on the farms, however. Here is a description of U.S. women's farm labor from the colonial era:

> From tending and slaughtering chickens, cutting and cooking meat, carrying wood, milking cows and goats, to making cheese, butter, candles, and bread,

growing and weeding vegetables, spinning and carding wool, often while pregnant or tending young children, she worked hard even into old age, when the
farm and its management may have passed entirely into her hands. Like her
husband, she engaged in trade and transactions with neighbors and townspeo-
ple (both male and female), kept notes (sometimes on the kitchen wall) and
sometimes recorded her work life in her diary. (Merchant 1989, 168)

Women's labor has always been as critical as the male "farmers'" for the
success of the family farm. Women not only worked in the fields but also
raised produce for their households, kept the books for the farm, tended to
livestock, and volunteered in local organizations (Fink 1992; Sachs 1996).
During the Great Depression, for instance, women's sales of eggs and cream
on the American Plains provided cash to keep family farms afloat (even
though the income women brought in was still seen as "extra" rather than
"real" money), and their gardens kept the family fed (Fink 1992). In addition, women did all the cooking, cleaning, and childrearing.

Today in the rural Global South, women's agricultural labor often entails
subsistence farming, in which women grow much of the food to feed their
families. This labor includes the sowing, weeding, fertilizing, and harvesting of the staple crops that provide the bulk of household's calories. These
women agriculturalists also prepare most of the food, gather wood for
cooking, manage the water supply, and do almost all the child care and
other household chores (Food and Agriculture Organization [FAO] 2011).
In West Africa, for example, 70 percent of agricultural production and food
processing is completed by women; however, African women own less than
15 percent of land, on average, as a result of colonization, which disrupted
female farming systems by both privatizing and outright appropriating land
to grow cash crops (Shiva 1993; Federici 2009).

So, who gets to claim the title of farmer? It depends on whose labor is
considered "productive." In 1800, women whose main work was caring
for families were considered productive workers. The household was the
main economic unit, and both women and men produced goods that
contributed to its functioning, such as furniture, housing, and food. As the
capitalist market grew, wage labor became a masculine pursuit. However,
for wage labor to be considered productive, women's household labor
had to be considered altruistic; thus began the process by which women's
household labor was devalued from an economic standpoint. By 1900 and
until 1970, nonwage household earners, including women and farmwives,
were categorized as dependents because they had nonpaying jobs (Anderson 1994; Folbre 1991; Bose 1984). In farming households, this meant that
official statistics only counted men's labor. This classification ignored and
discounted women's work in the household and on the farm.

This problem continues today. In 2012, the U.S. census counted 3.2 million farmers in the United States, 70 percent of whom were male. However,

male farmers made up 86 percent of the total number of principal operators, defined as the person who manages the farm and makes day-to-day
management decisions (USDA 2014b). Two-thirds (67 percent) of second
operators are women, of whom 90 percent are the spouse of the principal
farm operator (USDA 2014b) (see table 2.1).

Table 2.1.   Gender, Primary Occupation, and Years on Farm, 2012 (percentage)

	Gender		Primary Occupation		Years on Farm	
Farm Operators	**Male**	**Female**	**Farm**	**Other**	**<10**	**10+**
Principal	86	14	48	52	22	78
Second	33	67	37	63	31	69
Third	61	39	43	57	45	55
All	70	30	44	56	26	74

Source: USDA 2014.

Even if there are multiple operators, the person responding to the census
inquiry identifies the principal farm operator during the data-collection
process; sometimes the default is to name the man if a couple is farming,
even though both are working on the farm (personal communication,
Tamara M.). These data, then, obfuscate the distribution of actual labor
on the farm in favor of ownership and managerial duties, two skills often
associated with men and masculinity.

Women's labor, however, is still critical to the success of the family farm.
Women still work in the fields and take care of the household, but their
off-farm employment income often keeps smaller family farms afloat. The
share of women working off-farm has recently grown substantially, from 42
percent in 1982 to 59 percent in 2007 (Hoppe and Korb 2013), and wom-
en's work provides not only a steady income (farmers don't often get paid
until the harvest) but also health insurance and other benefits not readily
available to self-employed workers. It is possible that women's off-farm
work may not be entirely positive as this work is often low-paying service
work (Mammon and Paxon 2000) and may reduce women's involvement
and importance in farm activities even further (Saugeres 2002; Shortall
1999). However, official statistics only capture this labor if it contributes to
the household income.

A similar gendered classification process ignores women's agricultural
labor in the Global South. According to the Food and Agriculture Organization (2011) of the United Nations, women produce more than half of
all food that is grown globally. But again, this may underestimate women's
agricultural labor. In most urban agriculture household systems, for exam-

ple, men are responsible for a few cash crops and larger livestock, which generates income for the family, whereas women grow subsistence crops and tend small animals, a position that places them in charge of household food security and nutrition but does not officially make them "farmers" (Hovorka 1998; Sachs 1996).

Thus, women's agricultural labor continues to be underrepresented in national and global statistics for many of the same reasons we find in the developed world. Women consider their primary work to be in the home and don't often identify as "farmers"; also, women's subsistence labor is not considered farm labor by those in official government positions because it is not sold on the market. Given the importance of women's work to household food security, the absence of their labor from official statistics means they may not receive resources or training from development programs or government grants for local market development. If only men are officially designated as farmers, women may not receive important resources to help them grow food for their families or communities. In summary, the social construction of a farmer as the person who grows food to sell to others artificially dichotomizes market versus subsistence farming and values the former over the latter.

WHAT IS A FARM?

What is officially considered a farm is also a social construction with gendered consequences. Many people, a large number of whom are women, are active in alternative forms of growing food, including community gardens and urban agriculture (Glover, Shinew, and Parry 2005). However, it is difficult to find statistics on the number of gardeners or community gardens, especially if they do not meet the federal classification of a farm (an operation that produces and sells at least $1,000 worth of food in a year). Cultivation of food for subsistence or communities, work often done by women, people of color, and the poor, is not included in official statistics. Nevertheless, this work provides important food security for households and forms a resistance to the modern food system, which floods poor and minority neighborhoods with junk and unhealthy foods (Ore 2011). The 350 farmers who once grew food on fourteen acres in the South Central Community Garden in South Central Los Angeles may not have been included in U.S. Department of Agriculture (USDA) statistics. However, the food they grew supported their families and provided traditional foods not found in grocery stores, such as cactus and tomatillos. The garden space also united immigrants and residents in this low-income community. Unfortunately, developers razed the garden, including some fruit trees and bushes a decade old, when the city sold the land in 2006 (Kennedy 2009).

Another historical example of growing food for the community is the Freedom Farms Cooperative, founded in Mississippi in the late 1960s by African American activist Fannie Lou Hamer. In an effort to empower families disadvantaged by deep poverty and disenfranchised by the white majority, Hamer founded Freedom Farms to promote food sovereignty for her community (White 2017). Freedom Farms was an agricultural cooperative that included not only community gardens and a pig bank but also a Head Start program, commercial kitchen, garment factory, sewing cooperative, and a tool bank. Members collectively planted and harvested crops in the community garden. At the end of the growing season, 10 percent of the harvest was donated to hungry families whose members were unable to work, while the member families split the remainder. Even though the cooperative folded in 1974, it was a model for self-determination in food production and consumption. Hamer's perspective was that she might still be oppressed, but at least she wouldn't go hungry (White 2017).

This focus on growing food for the community rather than the market guides many of the current community efforts toward food security. Monica White (2011) profiled eight black, female urban farmers who grew for D-Town, an urban farm sponsored by the Detroit Black Community Food Security Network, an organization that promotes greater local participation in the politics of food production. These women, many of whom had full-time jobs, approached their work with growing food as a way to increase food security, promote food sovereignty, and show opposition to an economic system that marginalized their families and their community. These women viewed themselves not as gardeners but as activist farmers, and they believed that growing food also grows community and creates a safe space to collectively resist "the social, economic, and gendered oppression that complicates the accessibility of healthy food for poor people and the communities of color who have not left the impoverished city" (White 2011, 25).

These examples illustrate that the distinction between "farming," "gardening," and "subsistence" is an artifact of a gendered, capitalist orientation. The definition of a farmer as someone who grows food for the market does not include those who grow food in their yards or those who cooperate with others to grow food in their communities. Subsistence farming is often critical for household food security but may not get captured in statistics, as money is not exchanged. Gardening has been an important activity in many low-income and immigrant communities, serving as a tool not only for providing food but also for creating community and resisting oppression. The lack of scholarly research on household food growing is also a symptom of a gendered production system that only recognizes work done for the market as official labor. In more practical terms, this means that small farmers and gardeners have more difficulty obtaining funding, financial credit, and especially access to land to sustain these alternative forms of food production.

WOMEN FARMERS IN THE UNITED STATES

The addition of women's necessary productive agricultural and reproductive labor on the farm complicates the image of the single male farmer feeding 128 people. Women farmers, at least in the United States, are demographically different from men (although almost all American farmers are white, an issue discussed later in the chapter).[2] In the United States, the average age of women farm operators in 2007 was fifty-nine years, compared with fifty-seven years for men. Women farmers and ranchers are, on average, better educated than men farmers and ranchers, with approximately 61 percent of women principal operators listing education beyond high school, compared with only 47 percent of men principal operators (Hoppe and Korb 2013). Women-operated farms in the United States tend to rely less on big equipment and technology, a necessity in industrial agriculture. This may explain why the average size of women's farms is only 40 acres, while the average size for men's is 149 acres, and why three-quarters of farms operated by women reported less than $10,000 in revenue (Hoppe and Korb 2013).

Why are the differences between men and women farmers and their farms so pronounced? Why are women slow to enter farming as an occupation? This section identifies several obstacles to women's entry into the profession of farming, including the stereotype of farmers as men and farming as a masculine profession, discrimination against women farmers in access to credit and land, and the stubborn gendered division of household labor on farms.

Association between Farming and Masculinity

One barrier women farmers confront is the association between farming and masculinity. Farming is a very physical occupation: it involves operating equipment, working outdoors in the elements, handling animals, and dealing with weeds and weather, as well as managing a business. The traits associated with farming are often the stereotypically masculine traits of endurance, physical strength, and independence. Women are associated with the household and caregiving: to be feminine is to be a farmwife rather than a farmer. Although this association is slowly changing, masculinity is still the default gender identity for farming at least in the Global North. Consequently, when we think of a "farmer," we usually associate the role with a man and the farm with masculine space (Brandth 1995, 2002; Fink

1992; Leckie 1996; Liepins 1998; Shortall 1999; Peter et al. 2000; Pini 2005; Sachs 1996; Saugeres 2002).

One important aspect of the work of industrial farming is operating machines and equipment. Machines become a symbol of farming masculinity (Brandth 1995; Saugeres 2002). Lisa Saugeres (2002) argues "the tractor has become an expression for masculine power and spatial domination over women" (151). This stereotype and the associated symbolic strength of men and machines may be a barrier keeping women from farming. If machines are symbols of masculinity, then working on machines and heavy equipment is an act of gender transgression for girls. Parents or peers may sanction girls for expressing an interest in machines or farming. Standards of femininity, such as cleanliness and the absence of physical aggression, may keep girls from entertaining an interest in machines or farming (Brandth 2006).

These gender stereotypes can not only keep women from considering farming as a profession but also make it difficult to break into farming. Lacking technical knowledge is a serious disadvantage, as heavily used farm machinery tends to break down often. Farmers have to fix machines themselves or get the problem diagnosed quickly, as planting or harvesting is very time sensitive. If girls do not grow up learning these skills, it can be difficult to find educational spaces that are welcoming to women. Traditional cooperative extension programs, for example, focus on an expert delivering information in a lecture format, whereas women may need more hands-on learning (Sachs et al. 2016). Women are also vulnerable to derision or harassment if they are one of the few women in groups of men farmers.

The assumption that farmers are men even affects the design of farm implements. Sachs and her colleagues (2016) describe two examples of how this presumption works in practice. One farmer in the women's farming network they interviewed described the process of attaching a plow to a tractor, an action that required considerable strength to move a heavy three-point hitch into place. Women may not be able to complete the task due to the sheer physical force required by the design of the hitch. Another farmer described her frustration with equipment designed for male bodies, particularly a walk-behind tiller that required manual braking. This farmer had to use two hands to stop it—most farmers who are men only need one—making it very difficult to operate successfully (and safely). Due to these limitations, some women farmers often find ways to farm that require less physical strength and reliance on large machinery, such as organic farming, which is more labor-intensive (Trauger 2004; Trauger et al. 2008). This could partially explain why women's farms are often smaller and less mechanized (and therefore less profitable).

Even in the alternative agricultural movement, which includes organic and local agriculture, women still confront the association between mascu-

linity, leadership, and farming. Early in the alternative agricultural movement, men took leadership roles, while women were relegated to the grassroots level or support positions such as meal prep or clerical work (Sachs
1996; Meares 1997). While both men and women involved in alternative
agriculture expressed similar values motivating their involvement, women
expressed additional values that connected farming with a commitment to
family, community, spirituality, and place (Chiappe and Flora 1998). These
values may not materialize as organizational change without women in
leadership positions.

Men are also negatively affected by a masculine farming stereotype in
industrial farming. Farming is one of the ten most dangerous occupations
in the United States based on fatality rates (McCurdy and Carroll 2000; U.S.
Bureau of Labor Statistics [BLS] 2016a), with constant hazards including
machine accidents and exposure to chemicals. Farming is also a very risky
profession, as changes in both weather and the economy are difficult to
predict. If one's identity is tied to breadwinning and keeping the family
tradition of farming going, losing either can be personally devastating.
During the farm crisis of the 1980s,[3] for example, American farmers found
themselves in debt, and many had to foreclose on their farms. Facing the
loss of their occupation as well as the loss of land, more than one thousand
farmers killed themselves during the late 1980s. Even today male farmers
(including farmworkers, loggers, and ranchers) have higher rates of suicide
than individuals in any other occupational category (Donham and Thelin
2006).

The conventional farming masculinity, in which men's identities are
connected to what and how they grow food, may hinder their ability to
alter farming methods in response to changes in the economy. Anne Ferrell (2012), for example, found that tobacco farmers who were men in
Kentucky had a difficult time switching or diversifying crops in response
to the changes in tobacco allotments due to their gendered identification
with a particular form of farming, which left their households vulnerable
as tobacco farming declined. The connection between masculinity and conventional farming may also hinder men's participation in alternative forms
of agriculture. If one's masculinity is tied to productivity and efficiency,
then a farmer growing food organically (which requires less mechanization
and chemical inputs but also reduces yields) could risk being viewed as
not masculine. Organic and small-scale agriculture also involves more interaction between the farmer and people in the community, interpersonal
skills not often associated with conventional masculinities. Gregory Peter
and his colleagues (2000) found that organizations like Practical Farmers
for Iowa (PFI), a sustainable agricultural group, provided support for male
farmers to engage in alternative forms of masculinity. PFI helped farmers
create more open social networks, decreased their desire to control nature,

and attempted to shift their definition of work and success. An important variable in this shift was not just more sustainable farming but rather the ability to share these ideas and find solidarity with other men. PFI fostered a social environment in which men were able to support new masculine identities while also creating space for them to share power with women.

Discrimination against Women in Agriculture

The mechanization and chemical technologies that are now so integral to industrial farming may have decreased farmers' need for physical labor, but they have also increased the need for land and capital in order to grow enough food to make a living. Industrial agriculture favors men, who have greater access to both (Sachs et al. 2016, 11). Until 1850, women were not allowed to own land in the United States; until 1982, federal estate tax recognized women not as co-owners but as heirs and taxed them on this basis (Jensen 1986). Women often came into farming through marriage, as wives rather than principal operators (Sachs 1996; Fink 1992; Whatmore 1991). However, there are signs that this system is changing, especially in alternative and sustainable agriculture, where women are starting their own businesses (Beach 2013; Pilgeram and Amos 2015).

Discrimination by banks and government lenders has historically kept women (as well as people of color, as discussed below) from obtaining the financial resources that are crucial to farming. Operating a farm requires access to capital and credit for buying machinery and seeds, loans that farmers repay after the harvest. Without access to credit, making a living at farming is very difficult. In 2011, for example, income-support payments from the federal government to farmers totaled $9 billion (White and Hoppe 2012).[4] Recent lawsuits brought against the USDA in 2010 and 2011 proved a history of discrimination by the department against women, as well as African Americans, Native Americans, and Hispanics, in the acquisition and distribution of these payments. Women farmers filed a case against the USDA in 2000, *Love v. Vilsack*, which claimed that the USDA discriminated against women with farm loan programs through the Farm Service Agency. These farmers charged that officials representing these agencies outright refused to provide application forms to women or denied their applications by telling them that farming wasn't "women's work" and that they should leave it to their father/husband/brother. As a result of the *Love* case, which was heard in connection with another case against Hispanic farmers (*Garcia v. Vilsack*), the USDA created a $1.3 billion settlement claim for women or Hispanic farmers discriminated against in the allocation of farm loans from 1981 to 2000 (USDA n.d.). The USDA also started providing targeted loans through the Farm Service Agency for socially disadvantaged farmers, including women. However, commercial banks are still reluctant to give loans to farmers who are women.

Women farmers in the developing world have even more difficulty accessing resources. Banks and governments consistently deny them access to land, credit, and training and ignore women's role in subsistence agriculture for development projects (Carr 2008; Hurni and Osman-Elasha 2009). Landownership is critical for maintaining a successful farm; if women have to rent the land they tend, they cannot invest in upgrades or long-term projects and can be evicted on a whim. In cities, men have the first choice of any available vacant land, as officials view them as market farmers, leaving women with low-quality plots often located a considerable distance from home. Tending these less desirable plots requires that women farmers expend considerable time, physical effort, and money for transportation. And while lower-quality land requires more input to be productive, women have less access to fertilizer, seed varieties, tools, and pesticides than men, putting them at a double disadvantage for cultivating successful farms (Peterman, Quisumbing, and Behrman 2010).

Unpaid Housework and Carework

Even today, when more men and women are farming together and have more egalitarian marriages, a stubborn gendered division of labor still exists in which women are responsible for household caregiving, including child care (Barbercheck et al. 2009; Reschke 2012; Sachs et al. 2016). Farming is a time-consuming and difficult occupation, with nonstandard hours and on- and off-seasons. Many small farms cannot survive without the off-farm income usually earned by women, leading to a "third shift" for some women farmers: off-farm waged work, on-farm labor, and caregiving. In addition, many farmers are also involved in community and organizational activities, which could constitute a fourth shift (McIntyre and Rondeau 2011; Sachs 1996; Sachs et al. 2016). For farmers in the Global North, this could partially explain why the average age of women farmers is fifty-nine. As a result of the difficulty of combining full-time farming with caregiving, many women with an interest in agriculture wait until their children have left their care to begin farming.

Organic agriculture offers an alternative environmental and social philosophy in which care of the Earth and connection to others are farmers' primary motivators for growing food. Feminists had hoped that women's participation in organic agriculture would not only change farming practices but also reorder gender relations at the farm and household levels. However, the gendered division of labor in alternative-farming households has also been resistant to change. While women in sustainable agriculture may be more likely to share decision making and management of the farm business, they are still primarily responsible for household domestic labor in addition to their farmwork (Hall and Mogyorody 2007; Trauger et al. 2010).

Women's domestic responsibilities may also prevent women from participating in the alternative agrifood movement or other agricultural or political organizations (Meares 1997; DeLind and Ferguson 1999). Women farmers' capabilities are stretched thin as they attempt to be successful farmers, mothers, wives, and community members. As one organic farmer, who is also a mother, wife, and local agricultural organization president, stated, "I'm getting tired. And I want to farm. And I want to ride my horse. I mean, I was at a meeting until 11 o'clock last night. And that's [not uncommon], because you get caught up in this, and you can't help it. It's good stuff, and it's very exciting how things are happening, and the momentum. But it's just not sustainable either. So here we are, talking about sustainable farming, and I can't even keep my life sustainable" (Sumner and Llewelyn 2011, 114).

As more women begin to farm as a profession, the gendered division of labor in the household appears to be one of the most difficult barriers to dislodge.

WOMEN'S GAINS IN AGRICULTURE

The above barriers notwithstanding, women are making inroads in farming as a profession. More farmers who are women are engaging in new food-production strategies, including sustainable-production practices and smaller-scale farms with specialty produce and value-added products sold on the farm (Chiappe and Flora 1998; DeLind and Ferguson 1999; Hassanein 1999; Meares 1997; Liepins 1998; Trauger 2004; Trager et al. 2010). Women operated 18 percent of the organic farms in the United States in 2012 (USDA 2014a) and one-third of Canada's organic farmers were women in 2000 (Summer and Llewelyn 2011). In the United Kingdom, women comprise less than 10 percent of all farmers but make up half of all organic farmers (Buckingham 2005). Women now make up 40 percent of community-supported agriculture operators in the United States (Trauger et al. 2010).

Women are also building networks to support each other in learning agricultural skills and building new forms of business. The Pennsylvania Women's Agricultural Network and the Women, Food and Agriculture Network are two examples of organizations supporting women farmers (Wells 1998; Sachs et al. 2016). Farmers who are women are also venturing into businesses that support other women who are farming. Two farmers from Pennsylvania recently formed a company that designs and sells tools made proportionally to women's bodies (http://greenherontools.com). Globally, grassroots organizations, in particular La Via Campesina, are challenging the values of conventional industrial agriculture, with women in important leadership positions.

GLOBALIZATION, GENDER, AND
THE FEMINIZATION OF INDUSTRIAL AGRICULTURE

While it may be the case that (white) women are making inroads into farming in North America and Europe, global businesses are increasingly exploiting women of color as cheaper and more flexible sources of farm labor. Scholars describe this wave of low-paying employment as the "feminization of agriculture," a phenomenon in which women, particularly in the developing world, are hired for agricultural work at lower wages (Collins 1995; Barndt 2008; Barrientos et al. 2005; Dolan 2005; S. Lee 2010; Preibisch and Grez 2010). Women in developing countries have always done much of the work to grow food for their households, but now they are also engaging in farmwork for large corporations. This occurs especially when their partners migrate elsewhere for work. As Carolyn Sachs and Margaret Alston (2010) note, women's labor, especially that of women of color and women in the developing world, is overrepresented in jobs at the bottom of the agrifood chain.

Farmwork involves picking, spraying, processing, and transporting the produce and fruit grown in fields. These jobs are often called 3-D jobs: dirty, dangerous, and degrading. Laborers work long hours in the fields, often with few breaks. They have little protection from the elements and pesticides. Much of this work is repetitive and involves lifting heavy baskets or running machinery, which can lead to permanent physical impairment or death. Workers are often housed in substandard barracks and paid below-poverty wages. Even though workers doing these low-level jobs are exposed to toxic chemicals, they often lack basic health care and experience significant health problems. In many cases, they do not seek treatment for health problems that arise on the job because they could be fired without due process or deported due to their immigration status (Bauer and Ramirez 2010; Association of Farmworker Opportunity Programs 2012).

Although women form a smaller percentage of the permanent workforce employed in commercial agriculture (women comprise about 25 percent of farmworkers in the United States, for example), they often constitute the majority of the temporary, seasonal, and casual workforce. Additionally, women fill most positions in packinghouses and other value-added processing activities. Employers hire women to perform work that requires dexterity and efficiency, such as planting, picking, and sorting, due to the stereotype that women have a "gentler touch." Men, meanwhile, are hired for jobs running machinery and trucks or even lower management positions. This occupational segregation not only puts men in jobs that allow them greater job mobility and control of other workers (Collins 1993; Barrientos et al. 2005; Kritzinger, Barrientos, and Rossouw 2004) but also leads to a gendered pay gap. In the United States, for example, the average woman farmworker makes $11,250, compared to $16,250 for male farmworkers, partially because of the difference in occupational positions (Bauer and Ramirez 2010).

Deborah Barndt (2008) describes the gendered division of labor on a corporate tomato farm in Mexico. Employers chose men for managers, machine operators, haulers, sprayers, and equipment maintenance, while they hired women for planting, pruning, sorting, packing, and picking. Managers claimed that women are more dexterous, more efficient, productive, and compliant than men and that the former jobs better matched the skills of women. In effect, this ideology keeps women from working in better-paying jobs such as food transport or machine operation, which are the best-paid jobs outside management (Barndt 2008).

It is not just the farmer or landowner who exploits women's labor; it could also be the husband acting as head of household. Sharecropping is a system in which landowners agree to provide resources to farmers, who grow on their land in return for a share of the crop or a similar arrangement. Sharecropping families often utilize unpaid family labor to work in the fields to make a living. In researching immigrant sharecropping in the California strawberry fields, Teresa Sanchez (2015) found that male sharecroppers did not pay their wives or daughters for necessary and extensive fieldwork but did pay their sons market-rate wages. Women sharecroppers, in contrast, paid their sons and daughters equally and required adult children to pay household expenses.

While heat, sun, and pesticide exposure is dangerous for all farmworkers, women farmworkers face gender-specific health-care issues. Reproductive health care is nearly nonexistent in labor camps and on company farms. Where available, care is often unaffordable or inaccessible, as workers labor at least six and sometimes seven days a week. The long hours and hot conditions make it more dangerous for pregnant women to work. The lack of access to private toilets in the fields keeps many women from urinating during the long workday, which can lead to dangerous urinary tract and kidney infections (Galarneau 2013). Exposure to pesticides increases the risk of premature birth and birth defects. One study of California fieldworkers found that women exposed to pesticides in the fields raised children who at age seven had IQ scores seven points lower than those of mothers who had little or no exposure (Bouchard et al. 2011).

Women working as migrant laborers also face the threat of sexual violence. Assaults, harassment, and rape are ubiquitous in the fields and in labor camps but difficult to quantify because so many cases go unreported (Bauer and Ramirez 2010). In Salinas, California, farmworkers referred to one company's fields as the *field de calzon*, or "field of panties," because supervisors raped so many women there (Ontiveros 2003). This problem is especially egregious for undocumented migrants and guest workers who are employed by one farm, a situation that gives the worker no other options for employment.

One federal case in Florida recently brought to light this kind of rarely prosecuted harassment. The Equal Employment Opportunity Commission (EEOC) filed suit on behalf of five women farmworkers against Moreno Farms, Inc., a produce-growing and -packing operation in Florida, charging that the two sons of the owner and a third male supervisor engaged in sexual harassment of female workers in the company's packaging house. This harassment included regular groping and propositioning, threatening female employees with termination if they refused the sexual advances, and attempting to rape or raping multiple female employees. All five women were ultimately fired for opposing the harassment. In September 2015, a federal jury awarded these women $17,425,000 for sexual harassment and retaliation; however, they are unlikely to receive this compensation, as the farm subsequently went out of business (EEOC 2015).

In addition to working in the fields, women are also responsible for caring for children and completing household work. Individual employment contracts with large farms can make it difficult to gain access to on-site housing or child care, and fluctuations in residence and income can make it difficult to qualify for child-care services. Sometimes grandmothers, aunts, or siblings take care of younger children, while older children help in the fields. Often the living conditions in the housing camps are rudimentary—making dinner or cleaning can be a significant undertaking.

Corporations and Governments Exploit Differences

Nations and global corporations exploit differences and divisions within categories of inequality—race/ethnicity, citizenship, age, marital status, and motherhood—to generate profit (Sachs and Alston 2010). Deborah Barndt (2008) describes how women's work in the tomato industry is further organized according to age, race, and ethnicity. At the packing plant she studied, sorters and packers tended to be either local women or young women hired permanently to follow the harvest. These young women were often related to the male managers and of mestizo heritage, earning three or four times as much as field workers and enjoying better living conditions. Field workers, who earned the least and were most exposed to the harsh sun and pesticides, were often older indigenous migrants from the south of Mexico or local *campesinos* (peasant workers). All women who were farmworkers faced a triple burden: they were low-wage workers in their agricultural workplaces, subsistence farmers in their communities, and domestic workers in their own households. However, employers privileged some women over others for better paying and less dangerous jobs, exploiting racial and ethnic difference to maintain profits in the production system (Barndt 2008).

Using mothers as a temporary labor category is an increasingly common practice in agribusiness, as companies hire women for less pay but can also count on them to return to their home countries due to their familial responsibilities. Spain, for example, designed a guest worker program in collaboration with the Moroccan government to ensure that Moroccan strawberry pickers would not stay in the country permanently. The program provided minimum-wage jobs for nine months, offering priority hiring for the next season if workers returned to their home country. This program specifically targeted married women with children, on the assumption that mothers are more likely to be anchored by their children to their home country and less likely to stay than male guest workers (Mannon et al. 2011). Another instance of this corporate strategy is Canada's Seasonal Agricultural Workers Program, which targets Mexican mothers who work in the Canadian tomato industry by securing positions for the next season if they return to their home country. Currently women only comprise 2 to 3 percent of guest workers in this program. Women's participation rate is low in part because Mexico did not even allow women to work in this industry until 1989, and only single mothers were eligible until 1998 (Preibisch and Hermoso Santamaría 2006). Another reason is the entrenched gender ideology that positions men as heavy physical laborers; thus farmwork is not considered appropriate for women (although women perform much subsistence farmwork in Mexico). For these farmworkers—mostly rural, single mothers—employment options at home are severely limited but made more urgent by their need to provide for families. While these women report that they gain independence and confidence by supporting their families, their worker colleagues tend to view them negatively either as bad mothers for leaving their children or as sexually available (Preibisch and Grez 2010).

AGRIBUSINESS, POWER, AND GENDER

The farmers and farmworkers who grow, pick, process, and transport our food are at the end of a food chain in which corporate managers, legislators, and government agents make the decisions about what to grow. These economic and political actors control the production of agricultural inputs such as seeds, fertilizers, and pesticides, as well as which producers get government subsidies. This system is also increasingly concentrated into the hands of a few corporations and government agencies. This "food system hourglass" involves a large number of farmers and consumers but significantly fewer wholesalers, distributors, and retailers—and even fewer suppliers at the top. In the U.S. food system, for example, there are ten to twenty dominant corporate suppliers of farm input (seeds, fertilizer, and farm implements), 2.2 million farms, approximately twenty-five thousand food processors and manufacturers, approximately thirty-two thousand food wholesalers, and 300 million consumers (Carolan 2012). A few companies clearly have a disproportionate share of the power in this system.

A similar concentration of corporate production characterizes other parts of the agrifood chain as well. In U.S. livestock markets in 2007, four companies controlled 83.5 percent of beef production (Tyson Foods, Cargill, Swift & Co., and National Beef Packing Co.), 66 percent of pork (Smithfield Foods, Tyson Foods, Swift & Co., and Cargill), and 58.5 percent of broiler chickens (Pilgrim's Pride, Tyson Foods, Perdue, and Sanderson Farms) (Hendrickson and Heffernan 2007). According to a 2005 report by the Erosion, Technology and Concentration Group,

- The top ten seed companies controlled nearly 50 percent of the $21 billion annual global commercial seed market and nearly all the genetically engineered seed market.
- The top ten pesticide companies controlled 84 percent of the $30 billion annual global pesticide market.
- The top ten food retailers controlled 24 percent of the estimated $3.5 trillion global food market.
- The top ten food and beverage processing companies controlled 24 percent of the estimated $1.25 trillion global market for packaged foods.

The managers of these national and multinational corporations, which wield a disproportionate amount of power in the production system, are mostly men (Carolan 2012). Patricia Allen and Carolyn Sachs (2007) use government statistics to report that in the United States in 1997, women owned only 16 percent of agricultural service businesses, 20 percent of food manufacturing businesses, 21 percent of retail food stores, and 23 percent of retail restaurant businesses. Of eleven major U.S. industries, agriculture historically has the fewest women in management, whether as executives or administrators.

Executive positions are generally held not only by men but by *white* men, who make considerably higher wages than women or people of color. Figure 2.1 illustrates the breakdown in management positions by race and gender. White men hold 48 percent of all management positions in the global food-production system, while men of color hold 16 percent; white women hold 25 percent, and women of color hold 10 percent (Yen Liu and Apollan 2010). In terms of CEO positions, 75 percent of the CEOs in the food chain between 2010 and 2014 were white men, while 14 percent were white women. People of color represented just 12 percent of food chain CEOs (Yen Liu and Apollan 2010).

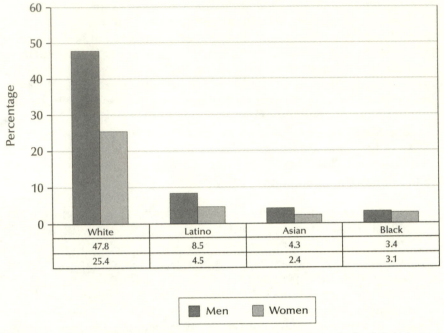

	White	Latino	Asian	Black
Men	47.8	8.5	4.3	3.4
Women	25.4	4.5	2.4	3.1

Figure 2.1. Percentage of people employed in managerial positions in the food chain, by race and gender (Yen Liu and Apollon 2011).

This discrepancy in executive positions by race and gender leads to income disparities. The annual median wages for white managers in 2010 was $38,000; for black managers, it was $33,000. As a point of reference for salaries, eight of the top one hundred U.S. CEOs work in the food system (which includes processing, growing, distributing, retail, and service). Together, these eight individuals were paid almost $200 million in 2012, a figure equal to the earnings of over 10,300 food service workers, people who are making and serving food in restaurants, cafeterias, and other food institutions (Food Chain Workers Alliance 2012).

Men also occupy other nodes of power in the production system. Corporate agrifood organizations are often overseen by advisory boards, which make decisions about business strategy and use their networks to promote the corporate interest. Unsurprisingly, in a review of seventeen food industry trade and front groups, men make up 85.8 percent of board members (Hamerschlag and Malkan, n.d.). Of the five largest organizations representing corn, soybean, wheat, cotton, and rice growers, which take in 90 percent of federal farm subsidies, female membership on these boards constituted only 1.3 percent (Karpf 2011). In contrast, of the top fifteen national nonprofits that focus on sustainable agriculture, women comprise 61.5 percent of employees and 60 percent of executive directors (Karpf 2011).

The federal government also plays an important role in the production system by shaping agricultural and food policy through the Farm Bill, an omnibus bill Congress votes on every five years. In current iterations of the bill, legislators decide which crops will get subsidies and other forms of government assistance. These subsidies include indirect payments for electricity or other inputs that contribute to the production process, marketing loans that guarantee minimum prices, and payments for leaving the ground fallow, among others. From 1995 to 2009, for example, the U.S. government gave out $211 billion in farm subsidies, most of which went to only a few of the largest farms in the country (Carolan 2012).

As with corporations, white men are also in control of the federal government. From 1917 through 2014, only 313 women had been elected to Congress, 39 of whom were women of color. In 2015, a record year for women in the U.S. Congress, eighty-eight women were elected to the House and twenty to the Senate. Currently, five of the twenty members of the Senate Committee on Agriculture, Nutrition and Forestry are white women, four of whom represent the (Democratic) minority party. This committee oversees almost all issues related to agricultural economics and research, including crop insurance and soil conservation, food stamp programs, human nutrition, rural development, and school nutrition programs.

Scientists also play an important role in agricultural and nutrition policy. Graduates of state agricultural universities work for government departments such as the U.S. Department of Agriculture, in finance and marketing (as food brokers), or as social science professionals (e.g., food inspectors). The research produced at these land-grant universities is disseminated not only in academic circles but also to farmers in the community through cooperative extension programs, which are managed and funded by the USDA.

Men have historically dominated these agricultural sciences, although this is slowly changing. In 1976, nearly all (99.6 percent) of agricultural scientists were male (Busch and Lacy 1983). By 1995, 86.9 percent of employed agricultural scientists were men (Buttel and Goldberger 2002). The percentage of agricultural-science doctorates awarded to women has steadily increased over the past forty years, from less than 1 percent in 1966 to 36 percent in 2005 (National Science Foundation [NSF] 2006). Today, women earn almost half of agricultural science degrees and comprise 17 percent of agricultural/food scientists, approximately 36 percent of biological scientists, and 17 percent of environmental life scientists (NSF 2006). At universities and four-year colleges, 32 percent of doctoral scientists in the agriculture, biological, and environmental life sciences are women (NSF 2006). In general, women have made inroads into the agricultural sciences in the academy and in government positions.

A cultural system that associates leadership and management with masculinity sustains and legitimates men in power. The connection between
masculinity, leadership, and agriculture extends beyond farmers to leadership in agripolitical organizations like the Farm Bureau in the United
States or the National Farmers' Federation in Australia and in corporations
such as Conagra or Monsanto (Brandth and Haugen 2000). The leaders in
these organizations are generally strong, determined, aggressive, risk taking,
knowledgeable, and (often) white, characteristics associated with a hegemonic masculinity (Pini 2005). These gendered expectations put women
(and men of color) at a disadvantage in achieving leadership positions.

The gender of the person who inhabits these corporate, academic, and
political positions makes a difference in leadership decisions and their
outcomes. In the sciences, women are more likely to support the paradigm
of alternative agriculture (Busch and Lacy 1983; Beus and Dunlap 1990)
and may have a more conservative approach to biotechnology (Buttel and
Goldberger 2002). Research from countries in which women are elected to
federal office in much higher numbers, such as Scandinavia and Rwanda,
suggests that women's issues are more likely to be mainstreamed when
more women are in legislative positions (Sainsbury 2004; Devlin and Elgie
2008). A more recent study finds that people report the highest levels of life
satisfaction in countries where women have greater political representation,
due in large measure to female politicians' support for policies aimed at improving social welfare and environmental protection (York and Bell 2014).

The race of political leaders also makes a difference in political and social
outcomes. White male politicians and federal agents in the United States
control access to capital and land through policy and oversight functions.
In 2012, African Americans owned and operated less than 2 percent of
American farms, Native Americans, 1.5 percent, and Hispanics, 3 percent.
In the case of African American farmers, this disadvantage stemmed from
discrimination by a combination of the USDA, financial institutions, and
landowners during Reconstruction until well into the twenty-first century.
Specifically, USDA agents intentionally denied black farmers loans after the
civil rights movement, which resulted in loss of land due to foreclosures.
In 1982, for instance, African American farmers received just 1 percent of
farm-ownership loans (Wood and Gilbert 2000). Without access to credit
and land, African American farms could not remain competitive, and
between 1900 and 1997, 98 percent of African American farms folded,
compared to 66 percent of white farms (Wood and Gilbert 2000). In
1999, African American farmers won a multi-million-dollar lawsuit against
the USDA for discriminatory treatment in decisions about who received
price-support loans, disaster payments, and operating loans. Hispanic farmers and women also won a discrimination suit against the USDA. This case
followed lawsuits against the USDA filed by black farmers for civil rights

violations in loan discrimination, which resulted in a second settlement in 2010 for $1.25 billion, and by Native American farmers, settled for $760 million. Since these lawsuits, the number of minority farmers has increased, albeit on farms with lower sales.

CONCLUSION

In general, food growing and processing in the Global North is dominated by corporations and big farms, which are controlled by white men. White men dominate management positions in food corporations and over-whelmingly make up the majority of CEOs, federal and state politicians, corporate board members, scientists, and even farmers and ranchers. This concentration of power is significant, as the people in these positions con-trol how we grow our food, who harvests and picks our food, and who gets public support for this endeavor. The outcome for the industrial food system is that we produce a lot of food, but much of it is only a few types of crops, such as corn, wheat, and soybeans, as well as a few types of meat.

White women in the Global North are growing more food as primary farm operators and are also involved in sustainable and local farming net-works that connect growing food to community development. However, they are more likely to encounter obstacles to growing food, such as dis-crimination in gaining loans or credit, from male farmers, or from a lack of time due to other family or paid-work responsibilities. An agrarian mascu-linity, which equates farming with breadwinning, control, and leadership, can deter women from entering the occupation but can also be detrimental to male farmers' health and/or willingness to try more sustainable farming methods.

A hierarchy in farming as an occupation exists by race as well as by gen-der. Most farmers are white, while most farmworkers in the United States are immigrants and/or people of color. Farmworkers do some of the worst jobs under hazardous conditions. Women farmworkers experience greater problems than men such as sexual harassment and violence, as well as a lack of reproductive health care.

So far we have discussed paid labor in agriculture. A gendered look at growing food reveals a material and ideological separation between work done for the market and work done for households and communities. Until recently, official statistics and common discourse divided labor on the farm between the "farmer" and the "farmer's wife" (coded as a dependent in the U.S. census until 1979), even though both were necessary to the success of the farm. Women worked in the fields (and still do), kept the books, and tended gardens and animals, in addition to cleaning, cooking, and caring for children. This labor is not included in official statistics, as only one person is allowed to claim the title of principal operator, or the person who manages the farm. And, of course, reproductive and caring labor is not included anywhere in official statistics.

This separation between market labor and social labor also divides growing food for the market and growing food for the family or the community. The former is considered "farming" and as such has the potential to receive loans, grants, and government funding. It is also available more often to white men and women. Food grown in community gardens or in backyards for subsistence is not considered "real" farming and as such does not offer the same access to resources. However, it increases food security for poor households, promotes social capital through community involvement, and in the developing world provides much of the household's main staples. Not only do we see discrimination in agricultural and processing based on gender and race, but the gendered division of labor and power continues in distribution and retail, the next stage of the food system and the topic for the next chapter.

NOTES

1. A recent study provides support for women's integral involvement in early agriculture. Anthropologists compared women's bones from the Neolithic, Bronze, and Iron ages with contemporary bones from female competitive athletes. The prehistoric bones were as least as strong as those of modern competitive rowers, suggesting that women were fully engaged in extreme physical agricultural labor, including tilling the soil, planting and harvesting crops, grinding grain, processing meat, and making pottery (Macintosh et al. 2017).

2. The USDA data suggests that women have made the largest gains in terms of groups entering farming as an occupation. However, methodological discrepancies may complicate this statistic. The USDA took over administering the survey from the U.S. Census Bureau in 1997. The USDA retroactively applied an adjustment for undercounting that increased the number of women in farming by 27 percent, which may or may not represent an actual increase in women joining the profession. In another methodological adjustment in 2012, the USDA estimated farms that may have previously been counted as nonfarms (Rosenburg and East 2018).

3. In the 1960s and 1970s farmers responded to calls from the government to "get big or get out" by borrowing for new machinery, land, and inputs to compete on the global market. Farmers planted and produced more food, which was successful as long as markets for that food grew accordingly. After the international financial crisis in the late 1970s and the embargo against Russia after their invasion of Afghanistan in 1980 closed off markets for grain, commodity prices plummeted, and many farmers could not meet their loan payments. This farm crisis resulted in a slew of farm foreclosures, especially in the American Midwest, leading to rural population decline and an increasing consolidation of farms. It also led to a wave of suicides by farmers who are men, which has not decreased since then. Possible

risk factors for suicide for farmers include job-related social isolation, potential for financial losses, barriers and/or lack of access to mental health services (especially in rural areas), and chronic exposure to pesticides that might affect the neurological system (McIntosh et al. 2016).

4. These income-support payments are also known as crop subsidies and include direct payments for growing certain crops, indirect payments for electricity or other inputs that contribute to the production process, and marketing loans that guarantee minimum prices, among other types of subsidies. From 1995 to 2009, the U.S. government gave out $211 billion in farm subsidies, 80 percent of which went to only 20 percent of farms (Carolan 2012).

CHAPTER 3

Shopping

If most people think they know about growing food, even if they just have a mental image of a farmer on a tractor, they are probably clueless about what happens to our food from the time it leaves the farm until it gets onto grocery store shelves or into restaurants. For most of history, directly after foraging for or harvesting food, humans ate it raw, cooked it immediately, or dried it for storage. In the contemporary food system, the food that grows on our farms rarely goes directly to the consumer and is instead handled by many people working for a string of food corporations before reaching our tables. For example, farmers sell their commodities[1] to corporations that aggregate this food and sell it to initial processors (such as Cargill and Archer Daniels Midland or even farmer cooperatives). Companies that provide initial processing then sell their products to manufacturers, who transform the food into canned vegetables, frozen dinners, and condiments. The food-processing and -manufacturing sector includes meat packers, bakeries, and consumer product companies such as Kraft Foods and Tyson. After that, the food goes to wholesalers, companies that purchase and store food products in a network of warehouse facilities and then sell and distribute them to retail food outlets and restaurants using an extensive transportation infrastructure.

But wait, there's more! The retail food sector includes grocery stores, convenience stores, vending machines, and other retail outlets where individual consumers buy food products for home preparation and consumption. This sector includes restaurants, fast-food outlets, eating and drinking establishments, and institutional cafeterias where individuals purchase both food and the service of having that food prepared and served. Who knew this step in the food system was so complex?

The distribution system is not only extensive geographically and logistically but also very profitable. As figure 3.1 shows, packaging, transportation, and wholesale and retail trade make up twenty-eight cents of every dollar we spend on food in the United States (USDA 2017b). The gender dynamics of this system, though, are probably the least researched aspect of the food system. While there is some work on farmworkers and processing (discussed in the previous chapter), there are very few studies of gendered processes in commodity food trading, wholesale distribution services, or transportation. Take trucking, for example. Currently most truckers are men, and the job, while paying more than service-sector jobs, can take a considerable toll on health and family life. Race is also a structural factor in the trucking industry in that people of color earn considerably less than their white counterparts (Yen Liu and Apollon 2011). This topic certainly deserves more scholarly attention. For the purposes of this chapter, I utilize feminist scholarship to examine gendered processes in food retail, one important part of the food distribution system (Koch 2012; Beagan et al. 2008; T. Deutsch 2012).

So how does gender figure into the story of food retail? Retail markets rely on gendered processes in at least two ways. First, women's labor in food retail is part of an inequality regime (Acker 2006) whereby organizations reinforce inequality through gendered and racialized hiring practices, race and sex segregation of jobs and hierarchies, and large wage differences. Second, retail relies on unpaid labor (often women's) through grocery shopping to complete the distribution cycle. As we'll see in this chapter,

Figure 3.1.   2015 food dollar (USDA 2017b).

white men dominate the ownership and management of the organizations involved in food distribution, while women and racial minorities dominate the low-wage service work in these stores. Shoppers, who are often women, are also responsible for the unpaid work of food distribution from the grocery store to the household. However, the grocery store is designed not to make buying food for households easier for the shopper but rather to maximize profit. This chapter looks at some of these processes, highlighting the gendered, raced, and classed ways in which these systems operate and the consequences for shoppers and people trying to provision their households.

GENDER IN THE SUPERMARKET

At the turn of the twentieth century, Americans had many outlets to acquire food. Public markets provided access to meats, fish, baked goods, and bulk grains and provided a more accessible distribution point for farmers. If food was purchased from a brick-and-mortar store, it was most likely a family-owned (mom-and-pop) store, which was the norm before World War II. These stores were very small and not necessarily clean or well lit, but customers were known by name, and credit was often the main form of payment (Humphery 1998; T. Deutsch 2012). They often sold in bulk and were an outlet for farmers' eggs and meat, with a limited assortment of packaged foods arranged behind the counter. At the same time many rural households also grew their own food, while peddlers supplied produce to urban neighborhoods (T. Deutsch 2012).

The supermarket changed this arrangement. The supermarket,[2] a self-service store offering food and household goods arranged and displayed by category, began its ascension in the United States in the early twentieth century in urban areas. Instead of selling a few packaged goods at higher prices, the supermarket sold a lot of products (high volume) at low prices. One way to facilitate more products leaving the store was to put the products in direct contact with the customer. In 1915, Clarence Saunders, the owner of Piggly Wiggly, introduced the first self-service cash-and-carry grocery store in which the customer could select her own merchandise from display counters and pay with cash (Bowlby 1997; Humphery 1998).[3] This move lowered labor costs but made impulse purchases more important since retailers' profits were now based on selling large quantities of food at lower prices than offered by small stores.

By 1960, due in part to increasing suburbanization and use of the automobile, supermarkets sold nearly 70 percent of all America's food (Humphery 1998). Today they are central to our retail system.[4] Supermarket sales in the United States amounted to $650 billion in 2015 (Food Marketing

Institute 2015). Even though we might think there are many of these stores, most are owned by just a few corporations. In the United States, for example, the top four grocery retailers in 2016—Walmart, Kroger, Albertsons, and Costco—controlled 39 percent of the market. The top twenty corporations controlled 63.9 percent of food retail in the United States (USDA 2015).

Consolidation is happening globally as well. In Europe, the top ten retailers accounted for 31 percent of the market in 2011 (Sandberg 2010). In several countries, the concentration is even more severe: Switzerland's top five grocery retailers represent 92 percent of the market, while in Sweden the top three companies, ICA, Axfood, and Coop, represent over 90 percent of the market (Sandberg 2010). Just two supermarket chains, Coles and Woolworths, control over 70 percent of Australia's food retail sector (Dixon 2008). Global food retail sales are about $4 trillion annually, with supermarkets/hypermarkets accounting for the largest share of sales (USDA 2015). Walmart is, no surprise, the largest global food retailer.

With the free market push of the 1990s, the Western supermarket model is even spreading into developing countries. By 2000, supermarkets occupied 50 to 60 percent of national food retail in Latin American countries; in South Africa supermarkets accounted for 50 to 60 percent of all food retailing (Reardon et al. 2003). This is a troubling development for poor consumers as supermarkets tend to displace local retailers and fresh markets as well as to drive up prices by replacing locally sourced food with more expensive packaged food (Dixon et al. 2007).[5]

The alternative food movement has spurred demand for healthier and local food, culminating in the revival of alternative food markets such as farmers' markets, community-supported agriculture (CSA) shares, and direct-to-consumer farm sales. Farmers' markets in the United States grew from 1,755 in 1994 to 4,684 in 2008 (USDA 2015). Alternative food networks have also increased in Europe; in 2003 an estimated 20 percent of farms in Europe were involved in direct selling via roadside stalls, pick-your-own operations, and farm shops (Renting, Marsden, and Banks 2003). While significant, this increase in alternate food retail outlets represents a small slice of the total food retail market and still relies on the unpaid labor of consumers.

PAID LABOR: SERVICE JOBS

The rise of the supermarket coincided with and partially enabled women's increased labor force participation. The supermarket excelled at providing packaged and quickly prepared convenience foods, which working women used to balance their expanding roles as workers and mothers (Goodman and Redclift 1991). As the supermarket model coalesced, women were hired for service jobs like cashier, baker, or florist, which required skill in interacting with customers, a stereotypically feminine characteristic. Managers and owners paid women in these positions less than workers in more masculine positions, such as butchers or managers, since it was assumed they were working for spending money, not as breadwinners (Barndt 2008). Today, the feminization of service work has spread through the food and retail industry in the form of part-time, nonunionized service positions (think Walmart). This, ironically, creates a deeper dependence on the food system to produce cheap food, since food workers are not paid enough to support their families (Guthman and DuPuis 2006).

In the retail sector there is an enduring and racialized sexual division of labor. White men comprise most of upper management and are overrepresented in jobs with heavy physical requirements, such as butcher and stocker, while women are hired for service jobs such as clerk and customer service. Today in the United States, men make up less than half the workforce in food and beverage stores but constitute 80 percent of supermarket managers. Of those managerial positions, 75 percent are held by white men. While women make up 60 percent of first-line retail supervisors, they hold only 18 percent of higher store-management positions and occupy many of the entry-level and low-wage positions. Women hold three-quarters of food-preparation positions such as supermarket deli counter worker, with a median wage of below $9.00 per hour. In contrast, men hold over 90 percent of the 150,000 butcher positions nationwide, with 25 percent of workers earning over $17 per hour (Center for Popular Democracy 2016). Women work on the supermarket floor in mostly customer service positions, such as cashier (Tolich and Briar 1999; McKie et al. 2009), which typically pay less than $13.30 an hour (Center for Popular Democracy 2016).

Even when men and women are hired as cashiers in the same entry-level position, managers often allow men to stock shelves and roam the store, while women are stuck at their checkout stands for the entire shift. Male stock clerks are able to learn more about the layout and workings of the store, a precondition for moving up the occupational ladder, and report higher job satisfaction (Tolich and Briar 1999). Cashier and customer service work is also physically and emotionally demanding. Standing in the same place for hours is physically exhausting. Managers record cashiers' performance down to the second with scanning technology, and cashiers are under constant pressure to maintain a quick and efficient pace (Tolich and Briar 1999; Barndt 2008). In addition to this physical task, cashiers must also engage in the work of presenting the "correct" emotions (cf. Hochschild 1983); they must be friendly and not show feelings of boredom or anger. Deborah Barndt (2008, 156) describes the skills necessary for retail service positions as "fast and friendly": employees at the checkout must handle both food and people with dexterity and interpersonal proficiency.

In addition, women's family responsibilities limit their advancement possibilities. A survey of British managers and cashiers revealed that women shop floor workers often take cashier positions, which they believe will allow them the flexibility to better combine work and family responsibilities. They often decline management positions when offered due to expectations of a conflict with their carework responsibilities (McKie et al. 2009). However, research by Jennifer Glass and Valerie Camarigg (1992) suggests that this notion of family compatibility is an illusion. They found that the people most likely to be in jobs compatible with parenting were men without dependent children.[6]

Gendered occupational discrimination is endemic to retail. There are specific allegations of gender discrimination against Walmart, the world's largest grocery retailer. According to the plaintiffs involved in a civil rights case against the corporation (*Dukes v. Walmart*), managers discriminated against women by not posting job openings, excluding women from informal all-boys networks, segregating women into female departments, and using stereotypical gender assumptions to justify putting women in lower-paid jobs (Featherstone 2004). The Supreme Court eventually ruled that the plaintiffs did not have enough in common to constitute a class and dismissed the case; however, these kinds of practices are not uncommon in most retail and service positions.

As cashiers are often judged on their interpersonal customer service skills, they are also vulnerable to harassment and sexual abuse by customers and management (Hughes and Tadic 1998; Gettman and Gelfand 2007). Researchers who studied levels of job satisfaction among employees at a mid-Atlantic supermarket chain found that 50 percent of the 2,519 females who responded reported some form of sexual harassment from their customers, and 40 percent reported harassment from co-workers and superiors, leading to lower rates of job satisfaction, higher rates of turnover, and lower job-performance scores (Gettman and Gelfand 2007). Joselyn Frye (2017), a fellow with the Center for American Progress, analyzed data from Equal Employment Opportunity Commission sexual harassment complaints between 2005 and 2015 and found that 13.44 percent of all complaints were from workers in retail trade, including grocery stores, second only to complaints from accommodation and food-service workers, at 14.23 percent.

UNPAID LABOR: GROCERY SHOPPING

Women are more likely to be scanning our food at the supermarket in low-paid service positions. They are also more likely to be buying that food. While the work of grocery clerks is paid, the work of consumers in grocery shopping is considered unpaid "consumption," a specific example of the market/household dichotomy inherent in the food system. If monetized, this work would add millions of dollars to the food economy. We can estimate how much now that personal food shopping is a new occupation. Instacart, a service that employs people to shop for your groceries, allows consumers to make an electronic grocery list and hires someone to shop at the store for them and deliver the groceries to their doorstep. According to Instacart's website, personal shoppers can make up to $25 an hour for this work (https://shoppers.instacart.com). The American Time Use Survey tells us that an average of 33 million people are shopping for groceries on any given day, and these individuals average forty-three minutes in the store (Goodman 2016). If we apply the $25/hour Instacart promises and assume the same amount of time in the store ([.75/hour shopping × $25 = $18] × 33 million shoppers), employing personal grocery shoppers would cost households $594 million a day! And this doesn't even include the additional labor of making the list or planning meals.

But food provisioning is much more complicated than simply going to the store, buying some food, and bringing it home. Grocery shopping is a skilled behavior that requires knowledge of the products available as well as the needs of household members. It involves simultaneously balancing household preferences and household budgets, monitoring inventory in the household, and improvising when necessary (DeVault 1991; Koch 2012). DeVault (1991) argues that shopping "means knowing both the local and abstracted settings, searching the market, making selections from among the alternatives available, and delivering the 'goods' to the home" (76).

Women are still doing much of the grocery shopping. In the United States, women make up 66 percent of grocery shoppers, and on any given day, 17 percent of American women are shopping, compared to 10 percent of men (Goodman 2016). Men are doing more grocery shopping than previously, whether as members of single households, as widowers, or, increasingly, as fathers. We don't have a lot of research on men's grocery shopping, but we do know that much of the grocery shopping for the household is still managed by women, who plan the meals and make the lists, even if they are not doing the actual shopping (DeVault 1991; Bowen, Elliott, and Brenton 2014; Hamrick et al. 2011; Beagan et al. 2008; Little, Ibery, and Watts 2009). Men may accompany women to the store to drive or help with bags, or they may take care of short-term shopping, like getting items for the meal that evening (Metcalfe et al. 2009).

Power in the Supermarket

Tracey Deutsch (2012) argues that one reason behind the success of the supermarket organization is that it curtailed women's power in the food retail environment. When women shopped at public markets or mom-and-pop stores, they often knew the shop owner and could bargain for lower prices, request specific items, or protest if they believed they were being treated unfairly. As chain stores took over retail space from independents, managers at a corporate office set standardized store policies and procedures that were the same in every store. These extralocal relations of ruling now controlled the retail environment (Smith 2005). In return for the loss of any say in organizational and managerial decisions, consumers were able to choose products for themselves.[7]

Not only did food shoppers lose the ability to negotiate, but managers and marketers perfected ways to intentionally disrupt the customer's shopping trip to the store in order to get her to purchase more than she intended.[8] Thus, there is a built-in antagonism between management and the unpaid grocery shopper; the shopper is often trying to feed herself or her family on a budget, or find healthy food, or shop during her lunch break, while management attempts to prolong her trip, win her loyalty, and get her to buy more than she anticipated.

Industry analysts advise managers to design the store to slow the consumer down and make her traverse the entire space, even if she only needs a few items (hence the milk is often located in the back of the store). Managers use lighting, smells, and visuals such as TV or cart screens to disorient shoppers and often rearrange shelves and move products at certain intervals to disrupt shoppers' routines (Patel 2012; Koch 2012). Managers place certain products at eye-level to entice shoppers to purchase them—sugared cereal typically appears at three feet, the level of children's eyes, while private labels are at five feet, four inches, the visual height of the average American woman—and mark up the price of impulse items at the checkout line. Managers also use loss leaders (selling products below cost to draw people to the store) and price flexing (varying prices in different retail locations within the same city without reference to real costs) to increase the sales of regularly priced products (Burch and Lawrence 2007). Food and nutrition experts advise shoppers to defend themselves against these retail strategies by writing a list, avoiding going to the store hungry, leaving children at home, and shopping only once a week, adding extra work for the shopper while making self-discipline a prerequisite for this work (Koch 2012).

Shopping and Femininity

Shopping can certainly be a pleasurable activity, and many people enjoy grocery shopping. It can also be an expression of identity (Zukin 2004) or an offering of love (Miller 1998; Cook 2009). It is additionally one aspect of how women and men "do" gender. Shopping is work associated with food and caregiving, both of which are linked to a feminine identity. When women shop for groceries for their households, they are "doing" femininity through their practices (West and Zimmerman 1987; DeVault 1991; Cairns and Johnston 2015). In other words, women are accountable for their food choices in the grocery store in ways that men are not.

Women often take on the responsibility of food shopping as an extension of their role as caregiver and can find it difficult to relinquish this activity since being a good partner/mom/spouse is predicated on the outcome of their actions. When shoppers describe why they do the grocery shopping, one common explanation is "It's just easier for me to do it." However, Brenda Beagan and her colleagues (2008, 668) argue that what appears to be an individual inclination is actually an expression of gender expectations. Women's work of grocery shopping is an aspect of a food femininity that makes women accountable to their households and families (Cairns and Johnston 2015). It is also work necessary to the food distribution subsystem.

Alternative forms of retail may exacerbate this tension between shopping, food, and femininity. While the majority of food is sold at a supermarket or hypermarket (Morrison and Mancino 2015), alternative markets are becoming popular, such as farmers' markets, CSAs, or direct farm sales. Shopping in these spaces can be more interactive and more rewarding than shopping in a supermarket. Farmers' markets, for example, are often public spaces in which community members can interact with each other and with growers. Research has found, however, that shopping and related foodwork in alternative markets can be even more labor-intensive for women (Cairns, Johnston, and Baumann 2010; Som Castellano 2015, 2016). For example, shoppers who use alternative food retail may actually spend more time shopping and procuring food due to the additional work of going to multiple outlets such as farmers' markets, CSAs, roadside stands, you-pick operations, food cooperatives, and natural grocery stores, in addition to visiting conventional grocery stores and/or growing food at home (P. Allen 2004). Shoppers also have to plan around the irregular hours these outlets are open, adding an additional layer of work in addition to the time spent on transportation to more than one venue. Research conducted on alternative markets in Ohio found that women who engaged in the alternative food retail system assumed a greater proportion of responsibility for planning meals and shopping than those women not engaged in local food systems, while men's responsibility for provisioning in these alternative networks actually decreased compared to that of men in the conventional system (Som Castellano 2015).

Combined with the cultural push toward intensive mothering (Hayes 1996), in which the mother is supposed to always be emotionally, physically, and financially responsive to their child's needs (regardless of her work status or her own needs), women's responsibility to keep their children healthy and safe through food purchases creates anxiety and stress

(Little, Ibery, and Watts 2009; McIntyre and Rondeau 2011; Som Castellano 2015, 2016; Cairns, Johnston, and Mackendrick 2013; Mackendrick 2014; Organo, Head, and Waitt 2013). Interviews with Canadian farm women highlight the stress that mothers, even those who are also involved in food production, experience when they are not able to live up to expectations to provide fresh, locally sourced foods (McIntyre and Rondeau 2011, 121).

Norah Mackendrick (2014) interviewed twenty-five mothers in depth about their work in the process she calls "precautionary consumption." This process enlists the consumer to engage in consumption practices that minimize the avoidance of toxins in consumer goods as a way to "shop our way to safety" (Szasz 2007). Mothers in more privileged positions can purchase products that minimize their kids' exposure to toxins from food and other products as a means to protect them from harm and regain some measure of environmental control and pleasure through consumption. Kate Cairns, Josee Johnston, and Norah Mackendrick (2013) describe a similar process, which they term "feeding the organic child," whereby "women think about the organic child as an ideal they should strive towards, and they position themselves as individually responsible for producing this child, through the provision of 'safe,' 'clean' food" (99).

As women take on the responsibility of buying healthy (or organic, local, or fair trade) food for their households, they also reinforce the neoliberal project of individualizing responsibility for collective problems as well as the connection between women, food, and caregiving (Cairns and Johnston 2015; Bruce and Som Castellano 2017). By ignoring the labor involved in shopping, the alternative market model shifts responsibility for the health and safety of the food to the individual shopper. Responsibility for effecting social change transfers from the institutions in the food system that have the most power—the state or the corporation—to individual household shoppers, who must shop defensively and carefully to avoid the toxic and unhealthy food produced in the food system (Som Castellano 2016; Guthman 2011; Koch 2012). In this scenario, the government has abdicated its responsibility to protect the health of its citizens, and the consumer becomes the monitor of what comes into the household, especially for children. Women, as the primary provisioners, are thus positioned as the primary protectors of health through their purchases.

Race and Class in Alternative Shopping

Scholars have also argued that aspects of the alternative food discourse and practice are raced (Guthman 2008a, 2008b; Slocum 2007, 2008). Not only is the regular farmers' market consumer in the United States a white, affluent, well-educated, older woman (Rice 2015), but whites also comprise the overwhelming majority of California's organic farmers (P. Allen 2004) and community-supported agriculture programs (Hinrichs 2000). As Slocum (2007) states, "Shopping local is often shopping white" (8).

This practice goes beyond just consumer demographics to include the process by which the values of local, organic, and fresh food—and the community created or imagined around this type of food culture—become the universal by which others are judged (Guthman 2008b, 383). Julie Guthman (2008b) found that managers of farmers' markets and CSAs portray their own values and aesthetics to be so obviously universal that those who do not share them are marked as "other." These values include romanticizing a European agrarian past of small artisanal farmers, which denies the farming experiences of African Americans in the pre- and post-Reconstruction American South (Alkon and McCullen 2011). As Guthman (2008b) notes, statements like "'Getting your hands dirty in the soil,' 'if they only knew,' and 'looking the farmer in the eye' all point to an agrarian past that is far more easily romanticized by whites than others" (394). Alison Hope Alkon and Christie Grace McCullen (2011, 939) also found this "white farm imaginary" valorizes the white farmer (and white consumer) but renders invisible the actual work of picking, sorting, and cultivating, which is predominantly done by low-paid Latinx workers. High food prices at farmers' markets also reflect white privilege in U.S. agricultural land and labor relations and whites' higher buying power (Guthman 2008a).

Social Class

Social class influences what kind of food one can buy, if it all. The U.S. Department of Agriculture (USDA) introduced the idea of food security in attempts to identify the number of households that can't afford or access food. These categories range from high food security (no problems with accessing food) to very low food security (multiple indications of disrupted eating patterns and reduced food intake). According to this classification, 15.6 million households (42.2 million people) in the United States are food insecure. The rates of food insecurity are substantially higher than the national average for households with incomes below the official poverty line (42.2 percent), households with children headed by either single women (37.2 percent)—almost three times the national average—or single men (27.6 percent), black households (25.7 percent), and Hispanic households (26.9 percent) (Nord, Andrews, and Carlson 2009). Food workers in particular suffer from high levels of food insecurity (Food Chain Workers Alliance 2012). While Americans overall spend about 10 percent of their budget on food, households in the lower income categories spend a greater proportion of their budgets on food. In fact, the bottom 20 percent of U.S. households spend roughly 35 percent of their income on food (see figure 3.2), leaving little money for other necessities, like rent, health care, or transportation.

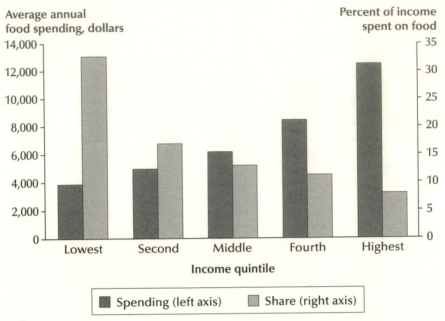

Figure 3.2. Food spending and share of income across U.S. households, 2016 (USDA, Economic Research Service, using data from U.S. Bureau of Labor Statistics, Consumer Expenditure Survey, 2016) (USDA 2017a).

Abstract categories like "food insecurity" can hide the lived experience of provisioning in these households. In a study of low-income women and provisioning, Sarah Bowen, Sinikka Elliott, and Joslyn Brenton (2014, 23) found that many shoppers, often women, did not have reliable transportation to get to the grocery store, which forced them to make trade-offs when they shopped. This mirrors government studies that found food-insecure households are less likely than food-secure households to drive their own vehicle and are more likely to rely on someone else's car or to walk, bike, or take public transit (Ver Ploeg et al. 2015). The mothers without personal transportation in Bowen, Elliott, and Brenton's study could only make it to the store once a month (when they could borrow a car) and often avoided buying fresh produce because it would spoil too quickly. Even in households with cars, the price of gas can also affect grocery shopping. Megan Carney (2015) describes shoppers going to the store fewer times per week or walking instead in order to save gas, which definitely limited how much fresh produce they could buy.

Irregular work schedules can also significantly affect one's ability to make it to the grocery store. Low-income families, many considered part of the working poor, are often employed in the low-paying service sector in jobs that offer nonstandard work hours and often necessitate working more than one job (Jacobs and Padavic 2015). Studies have found that one of the most important factors impeding low-income mothers' ability to provision is inflexible and/or demanding work conditions (Jabs et al. 2007). These parents often cope with time or income deficits by using convenience foods or skipping meals themselves. However, mothers in particular feel guilty and stressed about not being able to cook or provision more healthily (Devine et al. 2006). Ironically, food-service jobs are notorious for nonstandard work hours and inflexible schedules.

Several microeconomic processes, including the gendered wage gap and regressive tax policies, affect the household's ability to provision. Women's wages in the United States are, on average, 80 percent of men's. For women of color the wage gap is even more pronounced: black and Latina women earn about sixty cents for every one dollar that white men make. Roughly 12 million households in the United States (80 percent of the total number of single-parent households) are headed by single women, with a majority of these falling below 200 percent of the poverty line (Vespa, Lewis, and Kreider 2013). Households can receive Supplemental Nutrition Assistance Program (SNAP; formerly known as food stamps) and Women, Infants, and Children (WIC) subsidies from the government, but as the poor have little representation in Congress, benefits such as SNAP and WIC are subject to policy changes and are stigmatized as "welfare."

Even tax policies can have gendered consequences. Regressive sales tax policies, which are particularly prevalent in the American South, make food more expensive for low-income households. Katherine S. Newman and Rourke L. O'Brien (2011) detail the effects of a 10 to 12 percent consumer sales tax on low-income families, where $10 of a $100 grocery bill is significant to the family budget, especially at the end of the month. For these shoppers, it makes more sense to buy sugared cereal instead of fresh fruit because they know their kids will eat it, whereas the fruit might go to waste (Newman and O'Brien 2011, xxxvi). However, allowing kids to eat "junk" goes against current nutritional advice and can leave these provisioners open to claims of bad parenting (Elliott and Bowen 2018).

Contemporary efforts to address hunger and food insecurity may not make the work of provisioning easier. One of the main strategies policy makers have used to address hunger and food access is to identify food deserts. The USDA (2016b) defines a "food desert" as a "low-income census tract where a substantial number or share of residents has low access to a supermarket or large grocery store." Thus, one strategy to combat food insecurity (as well as obesity, as the two are often correlated) is to increase the number of full-service grocery stores in neighborhoods. However, supermarket access may not translate into eating more fruits and vegetables (Boone-Heinonen et al. 2011), nor does it necessarily help low-income shoppers provision for their households (Wrigley et al. 2002). Using super-markets as a proxy for healthy eating may also ignore other more accessible alternatives, such as ethnic markets or local vendors (Shannon 2014). Decisions about where to shop are influenced not only by geography but also by cultural, gendered, and classed associations with retail establishments (Bourdieu 1984; T. Deutsch 2012; Cairns and Johnston 2015).

Using supermarkets and neighborhoods as a proxy for healthy food may actually invert the causal relationship between food access, neighborhoods, and health. Instead of upper-middle-class people making better and healthier shopping decisions, grocery stores, businesses, green spaces, and other healthy amenities are located in these neighborhoods because of the demographics of their residents. Whole Foods's criteria for potential store locations, for example, include "good road frontage, plenty of parking, and . . . located in areas with disproportionately high incomes and levels of college education" (cited in Stewart 2009). Instead of adding more supermarkets as a solution, critics charge we need to confront urban planning decisions, social class and racial segregation in development, and the dominance of corporations and supermarkets in food retail (Guthman 2011; Shannon 2014). As Deutsch (2012, 223) found in her history of supermarkets in Chicago, the supermarket as a singular model for food retailing contributed to the significant decline in shopping options for poor people, as supermarkets could simply move out of unprofitable or difficult neighborhoods.

Social class even shapes which kinds of retail stores you find most comfortable (Pierre Bourdieu called this a "habitus"). The "foodie" shoppers Cairns and Johnston (2015, 47) interviewed described premium grocery stores such as Whole Foods as relaxing and enjoyable locations, while discount grocery stores were characterized as uninviting with an industrial feel and garish lighting. Women in disadvantaged class positions not only are denied access to certain retail venues due to a lack of resources but also have their femininity challenged by not shopping in the "proper" venues to support the health of their families. Thus, as femininity is tied to successful provisioning, women can feel they are failures if they are not able to shop in certain spaces or lack access to alternative foods, even when these options are not in their control. For those shoppers in poverty, just getting food into the household can be difficult.

Some communities and neighborhoods are working toward addressing the inequalities in retail and food access, building partnerships between municipalities, food pantries, and wholesalers to provide food. Milwaukee has a new mobile food store called Fresh Picks Mobile Market, which offers forty seasonal fruits and vegetables and meat and dairy items at thirty-six locations around the city. A long-running nonprofit in Oakland, the People's Grocery, provides not only food access, such as a mobile food market and a wholesale market where nonperishables are offered at affordable prices, but also programming for racial and social justice. This store also supports community leaders who will work toward strengthening community responses to problems (http://peoplesgrocery.org).

CONCLUSION

Food distribution, which includes wholesale trade, advertising, and retail, is a very profitable area of the food system but one of the least examined from a gendered perspective. In this chapter, I used examples from food retail to highlight the inequalities in this part of the distribution system. As in food production, (white) men are in positions of power in retail corporations and are more likely to be managers and owners of grocery stores and supermarkets. Women are overrepresented in entry-level jobs such as cashier and deli clerk, as well as in lower-level management, positions that entail direct interaction with customers but offer few opportunities for advancement, little decision-making power, and low pay. Women are vulnerable to sexual harassment in these positions, from both customers and from employers and co-workers, as a significant part of these jobs involve pleasing the customer.

On the other side of the conveyor belt, women are more likely to be buying groceries. This work is critical for households as it provides the ingredients to make meals, but it is also critical for the food system as it completes the distribution loop by moving products from store shelves into homes. This work involves more than just picking up products and putting them into carts. Shoppers must know what people in their households like to eat as well as their dietary needs; for some shoppers, staying within a budget is most important, while for others buying healthy food is the goal. Shoppers must manage the trip against any other constraints they have, such as work or transportation.

For many women, grocery shopping is one aspect of the work of caring for others and a means by which their femininity is judged. Discourses of intensive mothering and neoliberal individual responsibility intensify the anxiety of shopping for food for families. For some women this leads to precautionary consumption whereby shoppers attempt to protect their families from risks associated with industrial food, for instance, by buying organic or shopping in alternative retail spaces. For other shoppers, the lack of access to food is a major obstacle to provisioning their households.

In the store consumers have very little control over the process of shopping. Managers organize the space to maximize sales rather than support consumers in buying healthy food for their families. Marketing strategies such as product placement, advertisements, and shelf organization are designed to slow the customer down to spend more time in the store, as research has shown customers spend more money the longer they stay. In fact, the supermarket design took power away from the consumer as shoppers had more bargaining power in owner-operated stores or when buying produce from peddlers. Now, it is incumbent on shoppers to mitigate the problems of industrial food without any real power to make changes at the store or upstream. The next chapter examines how this work of shopping is connected to cooking at home, as well as how paid labor in restaurants is similar to the gendered inequality regime in supermarkets.

NOTES

1. In the industrial system, food that is grown for the market is called a "commodity" (Magdoff 2012).

2. The supermarket model of high volume and low prices extends to most stores in retail, including supermarkets, superstores, convenience stores, and discount stores.

3. Saunders came up with the name because the layout of the store drew the customer on a prearranged path, not unlike a pig run (Humphery 1998, 66).

4. The internet may be challenging the grocery store. Customers can buy groceries online through Amazon and have them delivered to their homes, while other businesses hire people to shop and deliver food to their door through online delivery services like Peapod and Instacart. While internet shopping is the fastest-growing segment of the food retail market, in 2016 it represented only 4 percent of total grocery sales (Danizer 2018).

5. There have been recent reports of the effects of industrial food on the health of consumers and especially children in developing countries as corporations expand into new markets. Supermarkets are one way to centralize the distribution of these products (Jacobs and Richtel 2017).

6. Thanks to Joey Sprague for this insight.

7. Of course, this process was not completely uniform. Black consumer cooperatives were critical in providing foods to black communities, and the 1970s saw a resurgence of the food cooperative model as an alternative to the supermarket. Other forms of resistance to this model are discussed at the end of the chapter.

8. The profit margin at the retail level is very small, less than 2 percent on average, so added or impulse purchases are significant.

CHAPTER 4

Cooking

Cooking is probably one of the most recognized parts of the food system, as many of us have either cooked for others or been on the receiving end of a meal at home or in a restaurant. Cooking in households includes the mental, physical, and emotional labor involved in planning, cooking, serving, and cleaning up after meals (Avakian and Haber 2005; DeVault 1991; McIntosh and Zey 1990). Cooking also takes place in institutional settings, such as restaurants, cafeterias (schools, prisons, etc.), and commissaries. This chapter examines cooking and serving food in both domestic and public kitchens,[1] in particular restaurants, as the research on other types of public kitchens is minimal. Femininity, masculinity, and inequality regimes structure this part of the food system much as they do the production and distribution systems. I start this chapter by examining the ways that domestic cooking, at least in the United States, is structured by gender.

FEMININITY, MASCULINITY, AND DOMESTIC COOKING

Domestic cooking and food preparation are almost universally associated with and done by women. The first food for most humans is breast milk. Women's work in feeding does not stop when babies are weaned, however. Cross-cultural data suggest that women have been primary food preparers for households and families. In a historical review of 201 cultures, anthropologists found that women were always or usually responsible for cooking in 186 of them, while in only 6 of these societies were men responsible for cooking (Murdock and Provost 1973). More contemporary data confirms this gendered division of labor is still the case: across developed countries, as well as in some prosperous developing countries (including China, South Africa, and India), women spent, on average, four times as much time as men on cooking and food cleanup per day (Miranda 2011, 25). In general, men do no more than 37 percent of the total household labor globally, which includes cooking (Hook 2006). Thus, women continue to perform most of the routine, everyday labor of preparing food and feeding the household.

It is worth noting that American men have doubled the amount of time they spend on household labor since the 1960s, while women have roughly halved their time spent in domestic labor, which includes cooking, as their involvement in the paid labor market has increased (Bianchi et al. 2000; Sayer 2005). The proportion of men who did some cooking for the household increased from 29 percent in 1965–1966 to 42 percent in 2007–2008, while the proportion of women who primarily cooked for the household declined from 92 percent in 1965–1966 to 68 percent in 2007–2008 (Smith, Ng, and Popkin 2013). UK time-use studies found similar results. Men's time spent cooking, cleaning, and doing the laundry increased from about twenty minutes a day in the 1960s to roughly fifty minutes a day in the 2000s, while women's decreased proportionally (Kan, Sullivan, and Gershuny 2011).

Even with these gains, however, women still do more foodwork in the household. In the United States, Canada, and Australia, women spend about twice as much time cooking and cleaning up as do men, often in addition to working a paying job (BLS 2015a; Australian Bureau of Statistics 2009; Statistics Canada 2015). In 2013, for example, 57.2 percent of all U.S. women were in the paid labor force, including 69.9 percent of mothers with children under eighteen (BLS 2014b). In the United States, women who are not in the paid labor force spend over seventy minutes per day preparing food, whereas women who work part-time spend fifty-three to fifty-six minutes per day and full-time working women spend thirty-eight to forty-six minutes per day preparing food. By contrast, American men spent on average between twelve and thirty minutes a day on food preparation, regardless of work status (Mancino and Newman 2007). In a study from the 2007–2008 U.S. National Health and Nutrition Examination Survey, of 3,195 adults at least twenty years old who had a spouse or partner, 36 percent of women reported the main responsibility for meal planning/preparation and food shopping, while only 7 percent of men reported taking the main responsibility for these duties (Flagg et al. 2014). Thus, domestic food preparation still constitutes a considerable part of women's second shift (with paid work being the first shift).

Sociologists have made considerable efforts to try to tease out why women are still doing the majority of routine household domestic labor (Bianchi et al. 2000; Brines 1994; Breen and Cooke 2005; Gupta 1999). One approach researchers have utilized to investigate household foodwork is to examine how gender is enacted in social practice (Connell 2005; West and Zimmerman 1987). This approach incorporates an understanding of the larger institutional and social order that shapes expectations for the accomplishment of gender; in other words, we "do" gender in our everyday interactions, and we know whether we are successful by the reactions of those people we interact with. Feminist researchers over the past thirty years, by utilizing a variety of qualitative methods, have amassed a significant body of scholarship showing how "doing gender" is central to the work of household food preparation and the continued (re)production of gendered identities and gender inequality (Murcott 1982; Charles and Kerr 1988; DeVault 1991; Warde and Hetherington 1994; Parsons 2014; Cairns and Johnston 2015).

In general, these studies find not only that cooking is an expression of cultural expectations for being men and women in a particular society but that individuals accomplish masculinity or femininity through cooking (or not). Michelle Szabo (2014, 21) offers two dichotomous categories to describe gendered cooking practices: "traditional culinary femininities" and "traditional culinary masculinities." These categories describe expected practices and subjectivities related to food preparation appropriate for men and women. For women, these expectations are connected to their reproductive duties in the household, while for men cooking is not expected or associated with taking care of others. I'll describe each of these in turn and suggest how these expectations lead to the continued gendered division of labor in households, as well as the devaluing of the feminine in relation to foodwork.

Culinary Femininity

Cooking as a characteristic of a traditional culinary femininity is an extension of the love and care women provide for their families. This work involves satisfying others' needs for nourishment and health, perhaps even at the expense of their own, and includes the anxieties and tensions involved in the routine accomplishment of this work (Murcott 1982; Furst 1997; Wright-St Clair et al. 2005; Cairns, Johnston, and Baumann 2010; Dixon and Banwell 2004). Cooking a "proper" meal, which is eaten in the household at a shared table, is essential to the production of family and home (Murcott 1982; Charles and Kerr 1988; DeVault 1991). Feminist researchers in the 1980s and 1990s found that women assumed primary responsibility for household foodwork and often prioritized men's and children's needs over their own.

N. Charles and M. Kerr (1986) interviewed two hundred women with preschool-aged children in the United Kingdom, analyzed their detailed food and drink dairies, and found that women identified the cooked meal, in particular a "proper" meal of meat and two vegetables, as central to the identity of the family. These women also defined their own food identities through the imperative to cook for others, using cooking to satisfy their husbands' nutritional needs to work as breadwinners for the family. Anne Murcott (1982) found similar results in her study of thirty-seven expectant mothers in the United Kingdom. These women again identified the "proper meal" (a cooked meal that includes meat, potatoes, vegetables, and gravy) as the key to women's successful accomplishment of domestic gendered expectations. Through the time and emotional attention she devotes to her husband's needs by preparing the cooked dinner on a regular basis, the wife expresses her domestic femininity and "does" gender accordingly.

In her classic study *Feeding the Family*, Marjorie DeVault (1991) found that food provisioning is a complex process of taking into account the needs and desires of others, as well as shopping, meal planning, and cooking. DeVault found that much of this food-provisioning labor was mental (and therefore invisible), involving attending to the tastes of family members, planning meals in line with the household's socioeconomic status, and negotiating the retail environment. Through the work of provisioning, and particularly creating meals that bring family members together, DeVault found that women produced the family and cemented their identities as mothers and wives. In the heteronormative family structure, foodwork is not only associated with women but made deeply personal as a place for women to display their emotional commitment to their families. This connection between food, femininity, and identity is difficult to modify, since rejecting or avoiding it implies a rejection of womanhood. DeVault (1991) states, "Women have been trained and encouraged to attend to others and to care for them, and to resist these lessons is to risk their 'womanly character.' Thus, for many, commitment to the work of caretaking has become an apparently 'natural' part of the gendered self" (119).

The Japanese packed lunch—the *bento*—provides a good illustration of the way that femininity and food appear "natural" but are really a product of "doing gender" (Allison 2013 [1999]). Japanese mothers are expected to send their children to school with a lunch that is nourishing and aesthetically pleasing, teaches Japanese food culture, and helps ease the transition from home to school. As these meals are eaten in public spaces, women risk having their femininity called into question if they fail to make a lunch their child will eat. Thus women spend between twenty and forty-five minutes every morning cooking, preparing, and assembling the *bento* and spend additional time during the day shopping, reading cookbooks, or discussing *bentos* with other mothers. While some may experience this labor as a creative outlet, mothers are accountable for this work and judged on their ability to make not only healthy but aesthetically pleasing *bentos*.

The *bento* reflects and reinforces women's (subordinate) position in the household as stay-at-home mothers, as the amount of time and effort necessary for these lunches is difficult to set aside while working outside the home. This example shows how cultural ideas about femininity are reinforced through interactions—especially with other mothers—which in turn shape a particular gendered division of labor. It also illustrates that when women do the work of feeding the family, they are simultaneously reinforcing their subordinate status in the household as well as reproducing unequal gendered relationships and family structures (DeVault 1991; Charles and Kerr 1988).

Scholarship from the 1980s and 1990s also identified an additional consequence of women's foodwork: the preparation and serving of food was a key instigator of violence against women in the home (Bell and Valentine 1997; Ellis 1983). R. Ellis (1983) discovered that a main reason some working-class men in a British study turned violent was that their wives did not have a hot meal ready when they came home from work. This finding remains salient today, as men still use cultural expectations of a food femininity as a justification for domestic violence (Counihan 2005; Hockey, Meah, and Robinson 2007). Bernadette, a participant in Carole Counihan's (2005) study of gender, food, and ethnicity of nineteen women and four men in the San Luis Valley of Colorado, described her experience of learning to cook for her husband: "Josè used to show me, he used to tell me, this is how you make the rice . . . but if I didn't get it right, oh, he'd beat me, until I got it right, really" (210).

One critique of studies from this period was their possible heteronormative bias as they only looked at heterosexual households with children (Beardsworth and Keil 1997). While studies on same-sex couples and households are still few, some suggest that the division of food labor may be more equitable in nonheteronormative households (Kurdek 2007; L. Mundy 2013). Christopher Carrington's (1999) important research on foodwork in lesbian and gay families uncovered some ambiguities, though, in how individuals in nonheteronormative households report their participation in cooking. In several of Carrington's interviews with men, couples interviewed separately said they were both the last one to cook dinner. In some of the female couples, both claimed the other person cooked dinner. Carrington suggests these couples were "doing gender," but in opposite ways. In the female couples, the partner who performed much of the feeding work tried to shield the gender identity of the less domestic partner by attributing more domestic work to her. In male households, the opposite may be the case; the less domestic man may try to protect the masculine status of the meal planner/preparer by taking credit for doing some of the foodwork when he really didn't do much cooking (Carrington [1999], 201). This research suggests the social construction of food and caregiving is tied to a gendered order in which doing carework through food is associated with a domestic femininity regardless of who is doing the labor.

Although women are working outside the home in greater numbers and the nuclear family is no longer the statistical norm in America, the centrality of preparing food for others as a means of successfully accomplishing femininity is still relevant today. Kate Cairns and Josee Johnston (2015) argue, "Food is powerfully connected to women's identities—to their sense of self as women, mothers, caregivers, consumers and citizens. . . . [F]ood is not just a hobby or a means to an end, but a key way to articulate and embody femininity" (158). Even those women who don't care about food or don't want to cook are still judged in relation to whether they successfully accomplish feeding others (as well as maintain body expectations, a topic for the next chapter). Women would be labeled selfish or worse if they cooked only for themselves, for their own pleasure, or not at all.

Rather than just a proper meal of meat and potatoes, though, women are now expected to cook or procure healthy meals with the right nutrition in order to produce healthy, productive citizens for society (Aarseth and Olsen 2008; Beagan et al. 2008; Cairns, Johnston, and Baumann 2010; Dixon and Banwell 2004; Meah and Jackson 2013; Parsons 2014; Cairns and Johnston 2015). This responsibility is reflected not only in what kind of food mothers are supposed to buy, as I reported in chapter 2, but also in the promotion of healthy eating and including "healthy" foods into family meals. Breastfeeding is a prime example. The American Academy of Pediatrics recommends up to twelve feeds a day, thus setting the standard by which babies should be fed (Murphy 2008, 216). Women who don't follow expert advice to breastfeed are subject to moral judgment if these food and eating choices interfere with the child's health. The choice not to breastfeed, especially if it privileges the woman's needs or is a result of structural constraints, makes the woman vulnerable to the charge of "bad mother" as one who endangers the health of her child through her feeding choices (Murphy 2008). This is just one example of how the association between food, femininity, and carework positions women (and mothers in particular) as the primary protectors of health.

Even as men take more responsibility for cooking, the expectations for femininity make it difficult for some women to relinquish the cooking role. Angela Meah and Peter Jackson (2012) use focus group and interview data with thirty-seven respondents and ethnographic observation with eight families in the United Kingdom to explore whether gendered kitchen practices are changing as men have started spending more time cooking and doing housework. In general, they found that while men are doing more in the kitchen, they are not constrained like women by gendered expectations for behavior. Women, they found, still feel responsible for monitoring what their kids are eating, as they know they will be judged on whether their kids are eating the right food. For example, one of their female respondents, Sally, described why she needed to remain involved in the household foodwork even though she was employed full-time. While her husband did most of the cooking and shopping, Sally found it unacceptable that he let the kids eat unhealthy crisps (potato chips). She decided that the children's packed lunches would remain her sole responsibility as dietary custodian. Of this, she said, "I feel it's my goal, my aim to make the packed lunches as healthy as they can be, and as exciting as they can be so that . . . I think that presentation and, you know, so that each night I sort of sit down [laughs] and sometimes it's easy and sometimes it's [not]" (Meah and Jackson 2013, 24). This example illustrates how the cultural expectations of food and femininity, enforced through interaction with others and refracted through discourse, sustain a particular division of labor in the household.

Cooking, Femininity, and Class

Social class also shapes food identities and behavior. Food practices and knowledge are a language for signaling one's social class. For middle- to upper-middle-class individuals and households, this manifests as a disdain for convenience and industrial foods in favor of organic and natural food, "authentic" food and home-cooked meals, and a cultural onmivorousness (Parsons 2014; Cairns, Johnston, and Baumann 2010). The ability to purchase and enact food knowledge is a resource that separates "foodie" women from those in lower classes, who often value tradition and frugality over novelty or exotic food choices (DeVault 1991; Naccarato and LeBesco 2012; Cairns and Johnston 2015). But gender is still salient in foodie households; women have less latitude to explore their own personal tastes due to the expectation to care for others. Kate Cairns, Josee Johnston, and Shyon Baumann (2010) state, "Women [tend] to describe cooking for others through ideals of care that prioritize the daily nourishment of the family" (605), while foodie men's cooking is not as circumscribed.

The salience of class is relevant beyond consumption knowledge. In order to cook, one must have a home and (at the very least) a kitchen with working appliances, difficult requirements for some families who are homeless or unable to rent consistently (Bowen, Elliott, and Brenton 2014, 23). Sarah Bowen, Sinikka Elliott, and Joslyn Brenton (2014) describe situations in which mothers cooked using only a microwave in hotel rooms or battled bugs and vermin in dilapidated housing in order to make meals. In addition to cooking space, time is also a resource that can prevent meal making. For some workers, "flexible" scheduling results in irregular work shifts, which can disrupt regular mealtimes. Food and retail service jobs are especially prone to irregular hours, and often these workers won't have the same schedule week to week. In essence, the ideal of the home-cooked meal and a well-planned lunch ignores the material dimension of provisioning.

In some cases, provisioning in low-income households can mean depriving some members of food. It is women who often sacrifice their needs for their children. They skip meals, wait to eat later in the day, or eat less so their kids can eat more (DeVault 1991; Carney 2015; McIntyre et al. 2003). To put food on the table, low-income women might also cut back on the size of meals served or go without three meals a day. As one mother stated, "Sometimes I would skimp or cut back a bit. I would eat, but not a very large portion for myself. But I wouldn't skimp with the child. . . . I would never allow her to go an entire day with no food. We wouldn't allow that!" (Heflin, London, and Scott 2011, 236).

In one study of twenty-five women who immigrated from Mexico and Central America to the United States and were feeding others in food-insecure households, Megan Carney (2015) found similar results. Her respondents often admitted prioritizing children's nutrition and health over their own, as expressed by the following statements:

- "I buy blueberries for my son, but I don't eat them because they're too costly."
- "I worry for [my children's] health. I give them more food than I give myself."
- "Pero mi hijo si come bien. Yo sometimes no" ("My son eats well. Sometimes I don't") (7).

As a result of sacrificing their nutritional needs for their children, women in low-income and food-insecure households are at risk of vitamin A, folate, iron, and magnesium deficiencies (Tarasuk and Beaton 1999). Women in these households are also at risk of becoming overweight or obese (Martin and Lippert 2012). Women in single-parent households are especially vulnerable, since these households are more likely than any other to be in poverty and/or face high levels of financial insecurity (U.S. Bureau of the Census 2009). This disproportionately affects black women, who are more likely than any other racial category to be single mothers (Kreider and Ellis 2011). Lynn McIntyre and her colleagues (2003) conclude, "Low-income lone mothers are compromising their own diets in order to preserve the healthier diets of their children. Although it may be that maternal self-deprivation of food is a socially acceptable practice, related to the gendered work of feeding the family and to the socialization of mothers who are taught to put their children's needs first, the implications for the nutritional health of women living in poverty are grave and go beyond the nutritional risks associated with their reproductive role" (690).

However, low-income women face more than just economic or physical disadvantage in feeding their families. Also at stake is the social necessity of being a good mother. Women's feeding activities are under constant surveillance by others, including individuals and institutions such as schools and government agencies. Poor women may be perceived as bad mothers or failed women if they are not able to cook the "right" meals or provide "healthy" food for their families (Parsons 2014; Brenton 2017). Putting this responsibility on women deflects from the material processes that cause food insecurity by making the unsuccessful accomplishment of feeding families an individual failure. The combination of the neoliberal focus on the individual and gendered expectations for caring and health makes it easier to target women for not living up to expectations rather than interrogating the outcomes of a lack of state support for welfare or questioning the food policies that favor food corporations over working families (Carney 2015).

Cooking as Resistance

While domestic cooking may support a traditional division of labor in the household and can be experienced as oppressive in some contexts, A. V. Avakian (2005) and Angela Meah (2014) remind us that for some women, especially women of color, immigrant women, and women from the Global South, foodwork can also be empowering. Oppressed women have used cooking as a means of maintaining control in unfamiliar or oppressive situations or of transmitting and maintaining their culture. bell hooks (1990) articulates the special space kitchens play as part of the "homeplace," that is, "houses that belonged to women, were their special domain, not as property, but as places where all that truly mattered in life took place—the warmth and comfort of shelter, the feeding of our bodies, the nurturing of our souls" (41). The kitchen, and the cooking that takes place within it, can also reinforce relationships between women—for instance, African American women used their own kitchens to create spaces of control and power separate from the white women's kitchens in which they worked (Wade-Gales 1997).

The Gullah—descendants of West African slaves who live in semi-isolation on the Sea Islands off the coast of Georgia and South Carolina—provide an example of the connection between women, cooking, and cultural empowerment. Gullah women's knowledge of food and cooking has played a central role in preserving cultural food traditions as well as maintaining a group identity in the face of economic development. Gullah women transmit group history and knowledge through their cooking and decide how much change they will allow to traditional food practices in order to maintain their West African heritage (Beoku-Betts 1995).

In households on the margin, women's cooking and marketing skills in the informal economy have played an important role in providing income to households and serve to illustrate the agency of women who struggle against gendered domestic norms and racial discrimination in the public workforce. Psyche Williams-Forson (2006) detailed black women's entrepreneurial practices during the late 1800s in the post-Reconstruction American South. Using their knowledge and skills in cooking and marketing chicken, black women set up food stands outside railroad stops, selling fried chicken, biscuits and breads, hard-boiled eggs, fruit pies, and hot coffee in pots, and used their earnings to improve the lives of their families. One descendent said, "My mother paid for this place [their home] with chicken legs" (Williams-Forson 2006, 32).

Drawing on *charlas* (conversations) with Mexican American women, Meredith Abarca (2006, 45) describes the importance of cooking not only in feeding their families but also in providing money to provision the family. Liduvina Velez remembers a point in her life when she turned to cooking to provide money for groceries to feed her own children. She moved her kitchen outside the front door of her house and sold tostadas, pozole, and *morisquetta* (white rice and meat) from a table she put in the street. These independent earnings and her corresponding increase in self-esteem enabled Velez to leave her abusive husband to better care for her children.

Immigrant women use their knowledge of food and connection to cultural traditions to maintain or enhance their status in new countries (Abarca 2006; Ray 2004; Avakian 2005). Bengali American women exercise religious power through the blessing of the food they cook in their kitchens (Ray 2004), and Armenian American women experience cooking not as an act of subservience but as a way to shape their identities as both Armenian and American (Avakian 2005).

It is important to note that the discussion so far has focused on the Global North, where much food is already grown and processed before it gets to our households. The infrastructure necessary to cook this food, which includes electricity, indoor running water, and trash removal, is accessible to most cooks in these countries. While it is tricky to make any generalizations about the conditions of billions of people on this planet, for the poor and those living in rural areas in the Global South, cooking is much more complicated. Fuel and water to cook with must be collected and transported by the household, labor that often falls to women and girls. Electricity is not always available, and cooking staples cannot be refrigerated or leftovers stored, making daily food preparation a necessity. Women cook as well as grow food, in addition to caring for children and the elderly. Gendered practices of serving men and children first can compromise women's health and, ultimately, household food security because women are responsible for both cooking and growing food (Hyder et al. 2005).

Even in these settings, women carve out spaces to use cooking to support themselves and their families. Women street vendors in South Africa interviewed by J. Wardrop (2006) were shut out of the formal labor market due to gendered assumptions that women don't work. However, in order to support their families, they found ways to sell food they made in their kitchens; in the process, they had to contend with harassment from government regulators, who made visits to ensure these enterprises were only temporary, and (male) customers, who occasionally became violent. Additionally, they faced logistical issues with hauling food from homes to the street and cooking without electricity. Their foodwork, however, provided the primary income for their families and elevated their status in the process.

Men, Masculinities, and Cooking

While a culinary femininity emphasizes women's nurturing and caring through foodwork, a traditional culinary masculinity approaches cooking much differently. Cooking could be used as performance, as adventure, as leisure, or even as seduction. Whereas women's cooking is associated with routine meal making, men's cooking is done as a special practice, which includes cooking as a hobby or performance or on special occasions (Adler 1981; Hollows 2003; Cairns, Johnston, and Baumann 2010; Szabo 2013; Julier 2013; Coxon 1983; Bove and Sobal 2006). Cooking at a dinner party, for example, is a way to cook for others but also an opportunity to show off culinary skills. Barbecues are another example of occasional cooking traditionally done by men. Instead of occurring in the feminine space of the kitchen, these masculine rituals of hospitality frequently focus on barbecuing or grilling meat in outdoor settings (Murcott 1983; Roos, Prättälä, and Koski 2001). Men may be able to enjoy their time in the kitchen at these parties or on weekends because their female partners have taken care of the necessary household chores such as child care, cleaning, or food shopping (Julier 2013; Koch 2012).

A traditional Western culinary masculinity is much less circumscribed or exacting than a culinary femininity. Cairns, Johnston, and Baumann (2010) found in their interviews with foodies that "men's narratives framed cooking as a leisure activity, even when they were also engaging in daily food preparation within the home" (605). One reason men may experience less stress when they cook is that meeting standardized nutrition requirements or cooking "healthy" is not a major aspect of a culinary masculinity (Adler 1981; Coxon 1983; Bove and Sobal 2006). Fathers identify a "proper" family meal as one their kids would eat rather than one with any prescribed expectations for healthiness or nutritional value (Owen et al. 2010; Metcalfe et al. 2009). This masculine approach to food and nutrition can have negative health outcomes for men, however, which I discuss in chapter 5 on eating.

In practice, there are indications of a new domestic masculinity influencing men's cooking (Gorman-Murray 2008). Qualitative studies involving heterosexual men have found that men are cooking to show love or to take care of others, including children (Bove and Sobal 2006; Lupton 2000; Owen et al. 2010; Szabo 2013). They are also able to negotiate new gendered identities around food as they take on more of the routine cooking (Aarseth and Olsen 2008). Sarah Daniels and Ignace Glorieux's (2017) analysis of a random sample of 1,768 Flemish (Belgian) time-use diaries in 2004 found that although women were still primarily responsible for household foodwork and at least one-third of the men in their sample did not cook at all, a third of their sample of 728 male respondents reported cooking out of obligation, necessity, commitment, and/or friendship, characteristics historically associated with a culinary femininity. These findings suggest that men's cooking is not unitary and may be in flux, especially for younger generations of men.

Another study of Canadian men suggests that a traditional gendered division of household cooking labor may be shifting. Michelle Szabo (2013) interviewed, observed, and analyzed cooking diaries of thirty Canadian men who performed over half the cooking for the household, specifically looking for the amount of food labor these men performed and their motivations for doing so. She found that while at least half of these men drew on "traditional culinary masculinities," which included experimentation and leisure as the motivation for cooking, some identified characteristics usually associated with a culinary femininity, such as cooking to show care and concern for household members. These participants "worried about the nutritional health and food preferences of loved ones, embraced the nurturing aspects of cooking, experienced both positive and negative emotions around cooking, and invested aspects of their subjectivities in providing 'proper' meals for themselves and loved ones" (Szabo 2013, 26).

Thus, participants who were the primary cook of the household and those whose cooking children and partners relied on were more likely to exhibit qualities associated with traditional culinary femininities, which suggests that a gendered division of labor still comes into play. However, men may experience a patriarchal dividend (Connell 2005) in that their labor earns them gratitude from women in the household precisely because they are exhibiting an alternative masculinity (Szabo 2014). Thus, men may benefit from domestic cooking in ways that women do not because men's cooking is still out of the ordinary and accepted as a gift—a process that paradoxically reinscribes a hegemonic masculinity.

A study of twenty-nine English fathers provides a general summary illustration of fathers' household cooking (Metcalfe et al. 2009). The fathers in the study engaged in cooking and shopping and incorporated foodwork as part of their identity as partners, and particularly as fathers, using it to show their commitment to the family. However, the majority of women in these households were still responsible for planning and coordinating the foodwork and the long-term planning of meals. The six men who did cook routinely were more often married to women who worked full-time or had a disability that prevented them from cooking. In effect, these men cooked out of necessity.

Cooking in Nontraditional Domestic Environments

While most research looks at heterosexual men in domestic settings, several studies have looked at men's cooking in nondomestic and/or same-sex spaces. These studies find that when men cook for other men or in same-sex spaces, they often try to distance themselves from a traditional culinary femininity. Jonathon Deutsch (2005) spent time with firefighters, who have to plan, shop, and cook for their mostly male co-workers at the fire station. He found that these men often provision in traditionally feminine ways—they are budget conscious when shopping, are concerned about food and health, and make an effort to cook pleasing meals. However, at their workplace and even in their domestic spaces, these working-class men attempted to distance themselves from any connection with femininity. During dinners at the fire station, they engaged in hypermasculine food talk, such as sexualizing food and women, and even though they were good cooks at work, they did not do any of the routine domestic cooking at home.

The Boy Scouts present another interesting case of boys cooking for other boys as troop members and sometimes for men as scout leaders. Jay Mechling (2005) found that the scouting program teaches boys to cook for other boys and men in their troop and that the skills promoted include making good food and enjoying food with others, which is a more traditionally feminine approach to cooking. Mechling argues, however, that the Boy Scout literature promotes learning to cook as a way to decrease males' dependence on women. It is not clear whether these cooking skills translate outside the camping environment into the household. For example, many of the skills Boy Scouts learn involve cooking over a fire; these lessons are directed not at preparing routine meals for households but rather at making food in the field.

Men who become widows or find themselves living alone often have to learn how to cook for themselves later in life. Lauren Williams and John Germov (2017) studied participants in an Australian cooking program designed to introduce cooking skills to male war veterans. Interviewing thirty men before and after the cooking classes, Williams and Germov found that men in the study did learn new cooking skills and were able to negotiate a new gender identity that included the practice of cooking. However, the characteristics they used to describe their new food identity centered on independence and self-reliance rather than the more feminine-coded qualities of caring for others or for oneself. In fact, Williams and Germov found that an important variable in these men adopting new cooking skills was the all-male classroom in which they could learn with and actually see other men engaging in work traditionally assigned to women. In all three of these studies, men who cook for or with other men attempted to distance themselves from appearing too nurturing (or feminine) by emphasizing traditional masculine culinary characteristics such as self-reliance, independence, and expertise and by minimizing feminine culinary characteristics that include caring for others.

In summary, while men are increasingly involved in cooking, they have entered the space of the kitchen largely on their own terms. In other words, they are choosing to cook rather than taking primary responsibility for the routine work of feeding the family, which still falls mostly to women. Meah and Jackson (2013) conclude, "While domestic practice is changing, there is little evidence in our research of a significant transformation in gender roles and relations amounting to the 'democratisation' of domesticity" (29). However, this research does suggest that gender hierarchies are being challenged in everyday practice; more research is needed on ways to encourage gender equality in the kitchen (Szabo and Koch 2017).

COOKING/SERVING FOOD IN RESTAURANTS

Historically, privileged women have employed or conscripted lower-class women or slaves to cook for their households. Even in the United States during the first half of the twentieth century, white middle-class women could hire domestic help, often women of color or working-class women, to do heavier chores, including cooking. As opportunities to work in factories and offices pulled women into the market, working women had to take on more domestic labor as part of the second shift or find a new group of women to employ. Today, many upper-middle-class professional women have transferred much of their domestic labor to immigrants (Tronto 2002; Hondagneu-Sotelo 2000). Even more families have shifted foodwork to the public market in the form of eating out in restaurants. In the United States, half of the average U.S. food budget is spent on food prepared outside the household (USDA 2016c). As of 2014, 32.7 cents of every food dollar spent in the United States went to pay for food services (USDA 2016c).

Restaurant work in general is one of the lowest-paying job sectors in the economy, and restaurant workers occupy seven of the ten lowest-paid occupations reported on by the Bureau of Labor Statistics (BLS 2014a). Over one-quarter of all U.S. workers who earned the federal minimum wage and almost 60 percent of all U.S. workers earning less than that are in food-preparation and service-related occupations (BLS 2015b). The median hourly wage for U.S. jobs in food preparation and service in 2017 was $9.70 (BLS 2017a).[2] This is significant, as over half of all food chain jobs

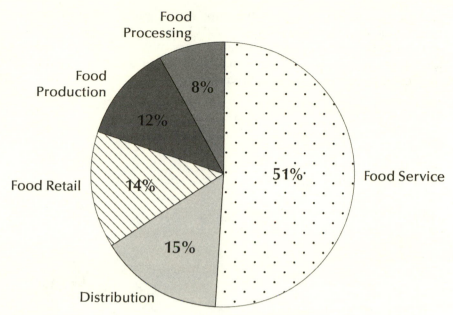

Figure 4.1. Food chain workers by sector (Food Chain Workers Alliance and Solidarity Research Cooperative 2016).

are in food service (Food Chain Workers Alliance and Solidarity Research Cooperative 2016) (see figure 4.1).

A gender and racial hierarchy exists in food service occupations. Fekkak Mamdouh and Saru Jayaraman started Restaurant Opportunities Centers United (ROC United) to advocate for and present research documenting the experiences of restaurant workers. In their reports, ROC United researchers conceptually divide the restaurant into sections based on placement and function of workers: the front of the house includes workers who interact with guests, such as hosts, waitstaff, bussers, and runners, while the back of the house refers to chefs, cooks, food-preparation staff, dishwashers, and cleaners. These spaces are segregated, with women working in the front of the house and men in the back. The back of the house is often further divided by race, with white men often working as chefs and head cooks and black or Latino men working as cooks and dishwashers (ROC United 2014; Sachs et al. 2014, 9).

Women occupy 64 percent of front-of-house positions, which involve serving other people (just as women do in the household). However, women make 76 percent of the average male wage, a discrepancy mainly due to differences in the types of restaurants in which men and women work. Women tend to be overrepresented in casual restaurants, especially in rural and suburban areas, where tips and wages are far less than in fine-dining restaurants (ROC United 2015). Figure 4.2 shows the gender distribution by industry; more women than men work in fast-food or lower-tier restaurants, an occupational segregation that has a significant impact on pay and working conditions.

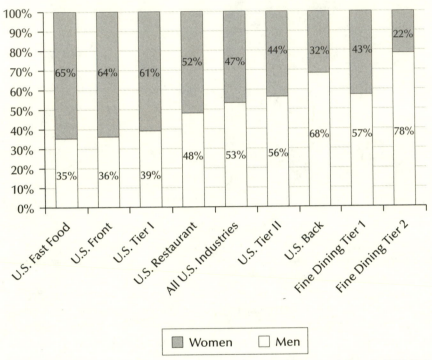

Figure 4.2. Gender segregation by industry in the United States and Canada (ROC United 2015).

In terms of pay, wages for white women are lower overall at $9.69 per hour on average, compared to $9.83 per hour for women of color, but both categories of women earn less than men of color, who earn $11.19 per hour on average, and white men, who earn $12.45 per hour (see table 4.1). The annual median earnings for full-time, year-round servers are $17,000 for women and $25,000 for men (ROC United 2015). Overall, both white women and people of color face the highest levels of segregation and the lowest wages. As a consequence, women in food service experience poverty at nearly three times the rate of American workers overall, while workers of

Table 4.1.   Average Restaurant Wages by Front-of-House (FOH)/Back-of-House (BOH), Gender, and Race

	White		People of Color		
	Male	**Female**	**Male**	**Female**	**All**
FOH	$13.91 (20%)	$9.73 (40%)	$11.69 (15%)	$9.95 (24%)	$10.94 (100%)
BOH	$10.80 (31%)	$9.51 (16%)	$10.83 (37%)	$9.51 (16%)	$10.40 (100%)
ALL	$12.45 (24%)	$9.69 (31%)	$11.19 (23%)	$9.83 (21%)	$10.74 (100%)

Source: ROC United 2015.

color experience poverty at nearly twice the rate of white restaurant workers (Shierholz 2014).

More than 2 million of these food workers are mothers—often single mothers who must support themselves and their children on $8 or $9 an hour. In a survey of two hundred mothers in five major cities, ROC United found restaurant workers spend 35 percent of their weekly wages on child care, leaving little after accounting for housing, transportation, health care, or even food (ROC United 2013). The structure of this work also makes it difficult for mothers to balance work and caregiving. As a service occupation, food service involves nonstandard schedules (shifts can change from week to week) and nonuniform work hours (often outside the standard nine-to-five workday) and lacks benefits, such as sick days or health care. For example, 55 percent of food service workers do not have access to paid holidays, and only 10 percent have paid personal leave (ROC United 2013). Mothers working in food service report missing shifts to care for sick children or having to forgo the more lucrative weekend shifts because child care is not available. These types of stressors, including spillover between work, caregiving, and nonstandard work hours, can also affect women workers' health in ways they don't affect men, for instance by causing sleep disturbances (Maume, Sebastian, and Bardo 2010).

Food service, especially front-of-house employment, also involves high levels of emotional labor and a focus on appearance, both stereotypically feminine attributes. The tipping system, which forces front-of-house workers to please customers to earn their wages, leaves many servers open to sexual harassment, not just from customers but also from restaurant staff and management.[3] A qualitative 1994 study found that seventeen out of the eighteen waitstaff interviewed said that sexual joking, fondling, and touching were common everyday occurrences in their restaurants (Guiffre and Williams 1994). Of 688 current and former waitstaff in thirty-nine states in a recent ROC United survey, 60 percent of women and transgender workers and even 46 percent of men reported that sexual harassment was an uncomfortable aspect of work life, and 60 percent of transgender, 50 percent of women, and 47 percent of men reported experiencing "scary" or "unwanted" sexual behavior. Forty percent of transgender workers, 30 percent of women, and 22 percent of men reported that being touched inappropriately was a common occurrence in their restaurant. A ROC United report stated that one in ten workers said they or a co-worker had experienced sexual harassment, which is probably a conservative estimate given that 37 percent of the sexual harassment complaints to the Equal Employment Opportunity Commission (EEOC) were filed by women restaurant workers, even though they only make up 7 percent of the total workforce (Jayaraman 2013).

As this research suggests, sexual harassment is widespread in the restaurant industry. Recently, women have been speaking out about specific experiences of physical and verbal harassment in celebrity and elite restaurants. Former servers at Mario Batali's New York restaurant claim he would grab their breasts, block their way through tight spaces so they would have to physically touch him to complete their jobs, or endure sexual innuendo and advances. One server said of him, "[Batali] wanted to wrestle. As I was serving drinks to his table, he told me I should sit on his friend's face." Surveillance cameras caught Batali kissing and groping an unconscious woman (Rosner 2017). More women will likely come forward about their experiences with harassment in this industry.

Men of color also experience discrimination in food service. Managers employ men of color to work in kitchens and other back-of-house jobs instead of in more visible work, such as waiting tables or hosting (Duffy 2005; Jayaraman 2013; Sachs et al. 2014). The more visible positions— such as wait staff and manager—tend to be dominated by white workers, while workers of color are disproportionately represented among those who remain in the back of the restaurant with fewer opportunities for advancement (Duffy 2007). Privileged men tend to be in positions of power; for example, 81 percent of management and 78 percent of higher-level nonmanagement positions, such as captain, manager, bartender, and head cook, are occupied by white workers (ROC United 2014), while black or Latino men disproportionately work as line cooks and dishwashers (Sachs et al. 2014, 9). This segregation affects wages. On average, men of color earn much less than white men, although they still earn more than women of all races (see table 4.1).

Chefs

Overall, cooking and serving food for others outside the household is low paying and low status, unless the restaurant is fine dining and has a position titled "chef." According to the U.S. Bureau of Labor Statistics, men comprise 71.9 percent of chefs and head cooks ("Chefs and Head Cooks" n.d.). Men's executive chef jobs are highly compensated with the average wage roughly $20.42 per hour and the highest 10 percent earning more than $35.00 per hour; in 2016, the average annual wage for chefs or head cooks was $32,864 for men and $26,989 for women (BLS 2012). In 2005, an industry survey found that men made up 89 percent of executive chefs, 82 percent of sous chefs, 66 percent of line cooks, and 60 percent of restaurant managers (Harris and Guiffre 2015). Of the 160 head chef positions in the top fifteen U.S. restaurant groups, women held only 6.3 percent (Harris and Guiffre 2015). Pastry making and salad prep are the only areas in which women held a higher percentage of positions than men.

The gender discrepancy in paid chef positions exists even as women are earning nearly 47 percent of BAs in the culinary arts in the United States. The latter figure is remarkable, given that women were excluded from kitchens and schools until well into the 1970s, when they were first allowed to enroll in the Culinary Institute of America, the most prestigious American cooking school. Deborah Harris and Patti Guiffre (2015) interviewed thirty-three women chefs who either worked or had worked in a professional kitchen to investigate why women are underrepresented in professional cooking settings. They found that women chefs confront stereotypes that they are not physically or emotionally strong enough to make it in the professional kitchen and have to prove themselves as "one of the guys," often by passing physical tests, tolerating sexual banter, and, unfortunately, enduring sexual harassment.

Harris and Guiffre (2015) also contend that because cooking is so closely linked to women and femininity, chefs experience "precarious masculinity" and must find a way to differentiate their kitchens from feminine kitchens and to keep women from taking over: "Men chefs have to defend the merits of their occupation in order to retain and increase the social status provided by their work, and by extension, themselves. In many cases, it is not that men chefs are necessarily trying to mistreat women. They are trying to resist the negative impacts that can occur when a male-dominated occupation transitions from being man's work to women's work" (2015, 190–91). Thus, professional kitchen culture tends to be hypermasculine, including an aggressive management style that often entails bullying and verbal harassment, a focus on displays of physical toughness, and a strict hierarchy of leadership (Nilsson 2013). Fine-dining restaurant kitchens are structured by the goals of manliness, which include "traditional masculine characteristics such as courage, fearlessness, endurance, pain tolerance, fighting spirit, strength and the ability to use force. Femininity is used to symbolize the opposite of these supposedly positive values in the restaurant" (Nilsson 2013, 661). This type of stressful environment, coupled with long work hours and often little time off, leads to burnout, health problems, and often substance abuse for many of the chefs, both men and women, who work in kitchens. Recent suicides of several top-rated (Michelin-starred) male chefs have started a conversation about the consequences of the way kitchens are managed, and groups like Chefs with Issues (http://chefswithissues.com) have popped up to support the mental health of chefs and restaurant workers.

Chefs in professional kitchens also promote a masculine style of leadership, with an emphasis on strength, competition, and not showing emotion in the face of intense pressure. To rise in the ranks, women face a double bind: when they assume a more masculine leadership style, such as being assertive, they are often viewed as unfeminine and rude; however, more stereotypically feminine styles of leadership, such as speaking nicely and encouraging cooperation, are not taken seriously.

Even more daunting, and one of the main reasons women leave professional kitchens, Harris and Guiffre (2015) found, is the difficulty women have in balancing work and family life due to the nontraditional hours and intense working conditions of the restaurant industry. A chef could be standing for twelve or more hours a day, repetitively lifting heavy pots and ingredients, and working most evenings and weekends—all elements that are not conducive to balancing household carework with employment. Restaurants do not customarily provide benefits such as health care or paid sick leave, which disadvantages women who become mothers, as they are overwhelmingly responsible for the children at home. Male chefs who become fathers rely on their spouses for child care.

The image of professional kitchens as masculine spaces is reinforced by media presentations of a "domestic masculinity" predicated on expertise and professionalism rather than nurturing or caring for others. Food shows often present men as professionals or experts, while women are featured cooking for others in more domestic spaces—think Emeril Lagasse versus Paula Deen (Hollows 2003; Swenson 2009). Men are also represented cooking for leisure or as a competition, both stereotypically male pursuits. These representations of "domestic masculinity" allow men to engage in a traditionally feminine activity without the connection to the domestic sphere or to caregiving (Swenson 2009, 51).

Even cookbooks reinforce traditional gender norms around foodwork (Adler 1981; Inness 2001; Neuhaus 2003; Rodney, Johnston, and Chong 2017). Authors of cookbooks for men create boundaries between men's and women's cooking styles. Men's cooking is represented as a hobby or in opposition to women's cooking (with a greater emphasis on meat, for instance) but rarely as a domestic action for serving others (Inness 2001; Neuhaus 2003). Alexandra Rodney, Josee Johnston, and Phillipa Chong recently conducted a discourse analysis of cookbooks by men chefs and found four culinary personas (with examples in parenthesis)—maverick (Mark Bittman), chef-artisan (Bobby Flay), self-made man (Guy Fieri), and

gastrosexual (Jamie Oliver)—each of which privileges professional expertise over domestic responsibilities. These personas reinscribe traditional
notions of a culinary masculinity oriented to professional cooking while
minimizing domestic cooking and caring responsibilities (Rodney, Johnston, and Chong 2017).

CONCLUSION

Cooking for and feeding others is closely associated with women and
femininity. Women are still doing much of the routine domestic cooking,
a gendered division of household labor that is reinforced by cultural expectations of a culinary femininity of caring for others through food. This
expectation can be difficult for some women to meet, especially those living
in poverty or working low-wage jobs. However, some women use cooking
to empower themselves and their families through maintaining cultural traditions or by selling food to provide for their households. When men cook
in households, expectations for masculine cooking are very loose; men have
the latitude to do it on their own terms and may even be rewarded for doing carework. There are signs, however, that more men are cooking for the
benefit of others and in more traditionally feminine ways such as by caring
for others and putting others' needs ahead of their own. Often these men
are the primary cooks in their households.

In the public sphere, women are cooking and serving food to others in low-
wage, low-status positions as fast-food workers and servers. The low pay and
nonstandard hours of these jobs make it difficult to cook for families. White
men benefit by working in more prestigious restaurants and positions and
are more likely to be in chef positions than women. These male chefs have
to work to distance this cooking, though, from feminine domestic cooking,
often in hypermasculine ways. Men of color are more likely to be working in
fast-food kitchens, while women and women of color are more likely to be
serving people for lower wages in less prestigious positions.

Again, the gendered separation of the market and the household and the
elevation of the masculine over the feminine disadvantage women in both
the household and the market. Women are more likely to be responsible for
cooking for others but at the same time are more likely to be in positions
that constrain their work in both spheres. Sexual harassment is prevalent in
food service positions, especially in those that involve serving others, like
waitstaff. Men are also constrained, in this case by a culinary masculinity
that values competition over caring and is reinforced by occupational environments as well as media representations. The next chapter shifts from
cooking to eating and explores how gender structures what we know about
food and the seemingly personal act of putting it into our bodies.

NOTES

1. Prepared meal services such as Blue Apron and Healthy Meal are interesting new alternatives to eating out. While cooking is still required, the meal is already planned, and the ingredients are specifically packaged for each recipe. Thanks to Joey Sprague for making this connection.

2. This statistic doesn't include other institutional kitchens such as hospital and school cafeterias, where women cooks earn an average of $8.72 per hour.

3. Federal law allows for pay discrimination between tipped and nontipped workers, permitting employers to pay tipped workers a subminimum wage of $2.13 per hour; 66% of all tipped restaurant workers are women (ROC United 2014).

CHAPTER 5

Eating

Although eating food is necessary for human survival, we don't eat indiscriminately. Societies set up rules that shape what is considered edible and inedible, pure and impure (Levi-Strauss 1964). Food is also a resource by which individual identities are constructed and reinforced, including gender identities (Beardsworth and Keil 1997; Bourdieu 1984; Counihan 1999; Inness 2001). This chapter examines the association between particular foods and gender, gendered norms for eating, and the linkage between food, embodiment, and identity. Gendered eating and nutrition can lead to negative health outcomes for individuals but can also create boundaries between groups based on other systems of inequality such as social class and race. I'll start with how gender influences what we choose to eat.

GENDER AND FOOD CHOICE

Gendered Eating and Identities

Why are more women than men eating at salad bars? Why are men more likely than women to grill meat? While the activities in these examples may seem like stereotypes, societies do associate certain foods with certain genders. In Western cultures, foods associated with women and femininity are "light" foods such as fruits, vegetables, pasta, and sweets, while foods associated with men are "heavy," a category that includes energy-dense foods such as meat and starches, which symbolize strength and masculinity (Bourdieu 1984; Sellaeg and Chapman 2008; Twigg 1983). The light/heavy split mirrors the body/mind dichotomy, in which the irrational body (including food and sexual appetites) are considered female, while the rational and in-control mind is equated with the male (Chernin 1981). The rational (masculine) person eats for power, strength, and without emotion, while emotional (feminine) eating is an attempt to control bodily urges through restriction and denial of hunger (Bordo 1993). Hence, the distinction between fruit and vegetables (light, insubstantial) and meat (strong, powerful).

The association between meat and masculinity involves multiple layers of meaning in Western society. Meat symbolizes men's strength and virility as hunters and vanquishers of animals and the natural world (Adams 1990; Lupton 1996). As men's work is associated with production involving manual labor, eating meat has historically been central to a Western diet. Meat is nutritionally dense, and eating it is an efficient way to fuel the body to create muscle and perform work-related tasks (Jensen and Holm 1999; Sobal 2005; Connell 2005). Recent cross-cultural studies confirm that this practice continues today. Men eat twice as much meat as women in Germany (MRI 2008, 44) and about 33 percent more animal protein in the Netherlands (Van Rossum et al. 2011, 54). A French study found that men consumed more protein, including meat products, than women, and this difference was larger among younger generations than older ones (Rousset et al. 2003). In general, masculine eating often entails foods that are now considered "unhealthy," such as meat, but more filling (Buerkle 2012; Sobal 2005).

Feminine eating, in contrast, is based on how much (or little) food women consume. As Kate Cairns and Josee Johnston (2015) note in their study of food femininities, even women "who care little about food construct their identities in a social context where idealized femininities are linked to skilled foodwork and successful body projects" (158). This idealized femininity includes eating in a feminine way, which is daintily, sparingly, or not at all. In other words, it is not "womanly" to have a hearty appetite for either food or sex (Counihan 1999; Vartanian, Herman, and Polivy 2007). In essence, masculinity is enacted through what is consumed, whereas femininity is enacted through what is not consumed; masculine eating is synonymous with power, while feminine eating is linked to weakness (Counihan 1999). This dichotomous eating starts at an early age. Girls are more likely to choose fruits and vegetables while boys are more likely to choose meats or fat-dense foods (Cooke and Wardle 2005).

As with any culturally enforced standard, individuals face negative consequences for rejecting eating norms. In research studies, participants perceived women who ate smaller amounts of food as more feminine; the more food women had on their plate, the less "womanly" they appeared (Mori, Chaiken, and Pliner 1987; Basow and Kobrynowicz 1993). Men who choose veganism are still considered less masculine and subject to criticism. Vegetarian and vegan men in Australia, for example, face disparagement, taunts, and other verbal sanctions for not eating meat, especially in homosocial settings like barbecues (Nath 2011).

It is possible, however, that unitary conceptions of masculine or feminine eating may not reflect actual food practices at the level of interaction. Jeffery Sobal (2005), for example, suggests the possibility that there are multiple masculinities, or masculine scripts, at work in everyday food interactions. The quintessential Western masculinity, the version that equates eating meat and protein with strength and virility, Sobal terms the "strong man" script. Other scripts include the "healthy man," the "wealthy man," and the "sensitive man." Sobal (2005, 147) suggests that men can draw on these scripts in different social contexts. For example, a man may eat burgers with the guys at work but a salad at home with a spouse. This might also be the case for multiple food femininities (cf. Cairns and Johnston 2015).

Food Choice and Social Status

Gendered food identities intersect with social class to further affect what and how people eat. Upper- and upper-middle-class men have more latitude to eat what are considered feminine foods (Bourdieu 1984; Roos, Prättälä, and Koski 2001). At the time he was writing, Pierre Bourdieu noted that working-class French men regarded fruit and fish as unsuitable foods for men, as they are foods eaten daintily. However, middle-class men had a larger range of food options, given their distance from manual labor and the cultural resources (cultural capital)—education, knowledge, and other skills—they possessed, which increased their status (Bourdieu 1984). In a more recent Finnish study, forty men from two occupational groups, carpenters and engineers, were interviewed about their daily food practices, health behaviors, and approaches to eating (Roos, Prättälä, and Koski 2001). The carpenters described food and eating as providing energy for work. They spoke of needing to eat meat as fuel for their bodies and thus avoided vegetables as not hearty enough. The carpenters did not talk about food in terms of taste or pleasure.

In contrast, the engineers favored vegetables and light meats and expressed concern about their health, reconfiguring what is traditionally a feminine approach to eating to account for their more sedentary lifestyles. They also talked about the importance of enjoying good food and wine on weekends and possessed a higher level of cultural capital, which distinguished them from working-class men and protected their masculinity as they made more "feminine" food choices (cf. Bourdieu 1984). However, both occupational groups emphasized that doing the cooking and talking about eating were still women's work (Roos, Prättälä, and Koski 2001, 53).

Foodies, people who devote themselves to food knowledge and exploration, are another example of intersecting food identities. Often middle- to upper-middle-class and white, they have the time, resources, and cultural capital to engage in food exploration. A main dimension of foodie culture is the continual search for exotic or unexplored dishes and recipes (John-ston and Baumann 2010). This quest for the exotic in foodie culture is a form of othering, or what Lisa Helkde (2013, 395) terms "cultural food colonialism." Searching for the new, the unique, or the unknown is akin to large-scale colonization, she argues, whereby the possession of the exotic, or even exotic knowledge, imparts considerable cultural capital to the col-onizer. Serving and eating Thai food cooked oneself confers uniqueness on the eater, who need not truly understand or have any contact with the actual culture in which the food was formed. bell hooks (1992) declares, "The commodification and appropriation of the Other has been so successful because it is offered as a new delight, more intense, more satisfying than normal ways of doing and feeling. Within commodity culture, ethnicity becomes spice, seasoning that can liven up the dull dish that is mainstream white culture" (21). The ability to go beyond stereotypical masculine and feminine food choices intersects with social class to allow more privileged eaters to transcend cultural boundaries as well.

EATING AND EMBODIMENT

Female Body Image

Gender, race, and class influence what and how one eats. These same forces influence how people think about and judge their bodies. For women in Western societies, when food was still scarce (up until the nineteenth century), the ideal body was plump and curvy (Beardsworth and Keil 1997; Mennell 1995). In advanced capitalist and even developing societies where food is abundant, resisting an excess of food becomes a measure of moral and social worth. Bodies, and particularly women's bodies, are expected to be thin and fit, a standard that projects attributes such as beauty, clean-liness, success, physical fitness, self-discipline, and health (Chernin 1981; Bordo 1993; Williams and Germov 2008). A thin body is a marker of feminine success associated with upper-middle-class women who have the time, resources, and access to personal trainers and medical advancements to achieve this ideal (Naccarato and LeBesco 2012; LeBesco 2004; Saguy 2013). The hegemonic thin and fit body is also a white standard, as other groups value body shapes differently. Canadians of African descent, for ex-ample, consider "thick" bodies healthy (Beagan and Chapman 2012), and African American women in the United States tend to view larger bodies as a positive ideal.

The hegemonic body ideal, though, is not really attainable. The aver-age model is 5'10" and weighs 107 pounds, while the average American woman is 5'4" and weighs 143 pounds (Bordo 2013). As a consequence of this pressure to remain thin—Kim Chernin (1981) calls this the "tyranny of slenderness"—women's relationship with food is often adversarial and begins at a young age. In a ten-year longitudinal study of adolescents and young adults, researchers found that at least 50 percent of the girls had dieted in the past year (Neumark-Sztainer et al. 2011). Extreme weight-loss behaviors such as taking diet pills, diuretics, and laxatives increased markedly between adolescence and young adulthood for young women and continued into adulthood (Neumark-Sztainer et al. 2011). Even women of "normal" weight tend to view themselves as overweight (Paquette and Raine 2004).

The thin body as a marker of white femininity and status is reinforced through overlapping institutions and social processes. The media and fashion industry bombard women and girls with four hundred to six hundred advertisements per day, often with images of supermodels, a body type attainable by less than 5 percent of the population (Paquette and Raine 2004). These images are increasingly unreflective of reality, as photoshopping of models' bodies creates images that don't or can't exist.[1] Susan Bordo (1993) suggests that not just the visual images in these advertisements but also the contradictory messages they send lead to cognitive dissonance in the female consumer. On one hand, women are supposed to display self-control and discipline themselves through diet and exercise to control desires and master their bodies. On the other hand, consumer culture promotes novelty and immediate satisfaction, which requires instant gratification through the purchase of new products. These indulgences require that consumers "treat themselves" with the new and the trendy, often unhealthy food and other products. Bordo (2013, 272) argues that this tension between indulgence and asceticism is a constant in women's lives and possibly accounts for the presence of both obesity and eating disorders.

Businesses certainly profit from this obsession with body shape and size. Not including weight-loss surgery, Americans spent $46 billion on weight-loss programs and products in 2004 (Lyons 2009, 77). Even though weight-loss programs rarely work and often exacerbate weight gain through the detrimental health effects of "yo-yo" dieting (Lyons 2009), and some products such as Fen-Phen have actually killed people, the weight-loss industry continues to grow. Weight-loss companies, government agencies, and the health-care establishment frame and benefit from obesity as an "epidemic" in which overweight and obese people need medical intervention to save their health and scale back on health-care costs for the rest of society, while at the same time obese people subsidize medical treatments and trials for the nonobese (Julier 2013; Campos 2004; Guthman 2011). This is a gender issue in that executives, politicians, and scientists are mostly men, while more women, particularly women of color, fall into the categories of "overweight" and "obese."[2]

Given the significant negative sanctions against fat bodies, it is no won-
der that women reinforce gendered eating norms. Sandra Lee Bartky (1990)
argues that women have agency and make decisions that in effect police
themselves and other women to adhere to the tyranny of slenderness.
Women actively sign up for Weight Watchers, elect to have plastic surgery
and other medical interventions, and restrict their own diets. Mothers pass
body anxieties on to daughters, and women transmit and reinforce messages about body norms to friends and co-workers, often in the context of
support for dieting and losing weight (Bordo 2013). Marie-Claude Paquette
and Kim Raine (2004) suggest that "by surveying and policing each other's
weight and through rewards and sanctions they give one another, women
perpetuate social norms of thinness. These monitoring processes are pervasive and strongly influential because they are seen as, and meant to be,
gestures of caring, friendship and sisterhood" (1053). Lauren Williams and
John Germov (2008) call this constant surveillance of women's bodies the
"body panopticon effect." Although this policing often takes the form of
praise and female solidarity (exemplified by the frequency of weight-loss
transformation features in women's magazines), the effect of these behaviors is one of division as women constantly compare their bodies to those
of the women around them.

Male Body Image

Although men report higher levels of body satisfaction than women,
societal expectations for men's bodies to be fit, lean, and muscular have
intensified. Media representations of the muscular male body have proliferated and possibly contributed to the 30 percent increase in rates of body
dissatisfaction among men over the past thirty years (Pope et al. 1999;
O'Dea and Abraham 2002). But masculine norms of hearty and fatty meals,
as well as the characterization of interest in dieting and body weight as
feminine, make it difficult for men to acknowledge they are trying to lose
weight or to diet when they are overweight. However, Amy Bently (2004)
cites the interesting case of the Atkins diet as a means to allow men to be
publicly conscious of their food choices without losing masculine status, in
large measure because the low-carbohydrate diet allows for protein in the
form of meat as one of the main components of the plan. The Keto diet,
a more contemporary low-carbohydrate, high-fat diet, could be a current
manifestation of this "masculinization of dieting" (Bently 2004, 35).[3]

Advertisers and marketers directly target men as food consumers. Media
images directed at men and their accompanying text symbolize food not
as a treat or temptation (as they often do for women) but as fuel for a
powerful body and eating as a rational activity to produce that body (Parasecoli 2005; Stibbe 2012). Advertisers market food to men by emphasizing

science and nutraceuticals (processed foods with synthetic nutrients), control of portion sizes, fat, and sweets, and convenient preparation. As Fabio Parasecoli (2005) notes, "A fit body becomes the material expression of one's dominion over the self, over the flesh and appetites that often appear as tainted by a definite feminine character. Control does not imply cooking; most of the dishes proposed in . . . magazines require little or no preparation. Cooking food seems to constitute a threat to the reader's masculinity; men consume, they do not get involved with the chores related to food" (35).

Not only do the media construct eating as a rational activity for men, but articles in newspapers and magazines suggest that concerns about nutrition and health are feminine attributes that men should not exhibit. In an analysis of men's diets in newspapers in the United Kingdom, Brendan Gough (2007) found that writers portrayed diet and nutrition as women's issues and described men as having narrow and unhealthy diets, knowing little about nutrition, and requiring "hearty" food to fuel their bodies. Articles presented men's cooking practices as special (e.g., novel, solitary, and selfish) and trivialized and mocked dieting, thereby reinforcing a dominant hegemonic food masculinity, one unconcerned with the preparation of food and the consequences of "manly" eating (Gough 2007). In fact, eating like a man involves keeping a distance from mainstream nutrition knowledge in order to maintain autonomy from it rather than engaging in the more feminine behavior of healthy eating (Lyons 2009).

FOOD, HEALTH, AND GENDER

Women, Food, and Health

Idealized body images and subsequent eating behaviors have different consequences for women's and men's health. Women's eating and bodies are constantly regulated and scrutinized; the combination of an intense societal pressure to maintain the perfect body and the ubiquity of gendered eating norms creates unhealthy levels of anxiety, which can manifest as eating disorders (Orbach 1978; Buerkle 2012). In the United States 20 million women and 10 million men suffer from some type of eating disorder during their lifetime, including anorexia, bulimia, binge eating, and eating disorders not otherwise specified (Hepworth 2008). Anorexia is arguably the most visible eating disorder and is more common among non-Hispanic whites in the United States; however, the overall prevalence of eating disorders, including binge eating, is similar among non-Hispanic whites, Hispanics, African Americans, and Asians in the United States (Hudson et al. 2007; Wade, Keski-Rahkonen, and Hudson 2011).

Bordo (2013) argues that the image of anorexia as the only or most significant eating disorder was cemented in mainstream culture when white women (or, rather, their middle-class families) became the first to seek treatment and their skeletal bodies drew empathy for those with the disease. This perception of anorexia as the most common eating disorder has consequences for those individuals who suffer from other types of eating disorders that don't necessarily lead to visible weight loss. Research comparing articles in the *New York Times* and *Newsweek* about eating disorders such as anorexia and bulimia versus articles about obesity and being overweight found that writers framed anorexics/bulimics as victims of cultural and biological forces beyond their control but blamed overweight/obese individuals for their body type and lack of control, even though some eating disorders, such as binging, can lead to obesity (Saguy and Gruys 2010). A. Saguy and K. Gruys (2010) argue that this type of reporting reinforces the connection between anorexia and victimhood, which is associated with white and middle-class women. This framing also blames the poor and people of color, who are overweight and obese in higher proportions, for their "excess" weight because they are not following the food rules set by the white mainstream. In effect, this framing renders cultural food rules that differ from white standards deviant (Strings 2015).

Becky Thompson (1994) dispels the myth that anorexia is the only type of eating disorder and that white, heterosexual, middle-class girls and women are the only people who suffer from eating problems. Thompson uses life history interviews with eighteen African American, Latina, lesbian, and heterosexual women to explore the causes of eating disorders, which she argues do not stem from vanity about self-image but are rather survival strategies for dealing with inequalities women face in their everyday lives. Eating and binge eating become a means for people to control one part of their lives, which are disrupted in many other ways including sexual abuse, poverty, and neglect. Binging on food can produce the same psychological effects as sedatives, such as decreasing anxiety and inducing sleep; keeping emotions subjugated to the physical realm of food can be a way to deflect thoughts from everyday trauma. But why use food? As many of the women in Thompson's study discussed, they were often young girls or teenagers when they experienced abuse and neglect, and food was easily available as a way to self-medicate when drugs were not. As women grow older, food disorders become a coping mechanism that is easy to hide and doesn't interfere with their caregiving responsibilities, unlike drugs or alcohol.

Food is also used as a coping mechanism for dealing with the effects of systemic racism and sexism. Tamara Beauboeuf-Lefontant (2009) interviewed fifty-eight black women to explore how the myth of the strong black woman as invulnerable affects individual black women. Beauboeuf-

Lefontant (2009) suggests that some black women use food as a means to suppress anger and/or deal with the multitude of expectations they shoulder to be strong and nurturing. In other words, food becomes a coping mechanism for "emotional states that have no direct mode of expression" (44). Women can evade criticism for overeating in African American communities for several reasons, including the aesthetic preference for thick rather than thin bodies, a view of dieting as a white endeavor, and beauty ideals more centered on hair texture and skin color than on weight. As one young woman in her study summarizes, "It's not because we overweight that we got heart problems, and heart failures and high blood pressure. It's 'cause we stressed out! And we don't know how to vent it the right way. Or, if we vent it, we vent it with a Haagen-Dazs ice cream or some other ice cream" (46). Weight gain for black women can thus be a protective response to the objectification and sexualizing of women's bodies by adding protective layers against sexual abuse, assault, and other traumas.

Men, Food, and Health

Men, especially gay men, are experiencing increasing rates of eating disorders as well. Gay men tend to idealize a leaner body shape, are more concerned about their weight, and report a greater fear of becoming fat (Yelland and Tiggemann 2003). They also tend to have higher rates of body dissatisfaction and eating disorders (Beren et al. 1996; Siever 1994; Strong et al. 2000; Williamson and Hartley 1998). One study reported the proportion of gay and bisexual men with symptoms related to disordered eating was ten times higher than that of heterosexual men (10 and 1 percent, respectively) (Strong et al. 2000). Eating, homosexuality, and body image thus present an interesting case of how food, masculinity, and embodiment are formulated.

Men also experience negative health outcomes as a result of a gendered orientation to eating. As a concern with health is constructed as a feminine attribute, which usually requires eating smaller meals and more fruits and vegetables, men are expected to be unconcerned with nutrition and eating "healthy" (feminine) food (Gough 2007; Jensen and Holm 1999). Eating "manly" foods like meat, though, can lead to such illnesses as heart disease and cancer, conditions which account for 50 percent of all deaths for men in all racial/ethnic categories and which some health experts attribute to an excess of saturated animal fats in the human diet (Courtenay 2000). A heavy meat-based diet may also lead to high blood pressure, which is a key contributor to heart attacks and strokes. Hence, medical experts advise patients to reduce animal fats and all highly refined foods in their diet and to increase their consumption of plant-based foods. If a hegemonic masculinity is related to a wide range of negative health behaviors, including excess meat eating and reliance on convenience foods (Courtenay 2000), then gendered expectations and norms for masculine eating may make it more difficult to change food behaviors that contribute to negative health outcomes. Life expectancy for men in the United States, for example, is five years less than for women.

Masculine eating norms can make it more difficult to recover from illness. A review of the literature looking at the diets of men in Western cultures after a prostate cancer diagnosis found that men rarely changed what they ate, even when advised by doctors that such a change was critical to recovery. The few men who did radically alter their diet (going vegetarian or organic) protected their masculinity by framing the changes in terms of an individual, autonomous choice rather than signaling that they were following nutrition guidelines or a doctor's advice (Mroz et al. 2011). A Canadian study identified similar framing strategies among men who live alone. While the men in this study articulated more traditionally feminine ideals about food and healthy eating, they simultaneously linked their ability to cook with traditionally masculine values of independence, self-sufficiency, and impressing women. They also had low motivation to cook for themselves, and their cooking focused more on entertainment and fun outside the domestic realm (Sellaeg and Chapman 2008). This research echoes Sobal's (2005) observation that "manly" eating frequently represents a way for men to enact masculine values of "independence" and "autonomy" by refusing to allow others, such as governments or spouses, to tell them what to eat.

GENDER AND NUTRITION

What we know about food, or nutrition knowledge, is a social construct (Biltekoff 2013). Mainstream Western food knowledge is based on a particular system of knowing (epistemology) that structures not only the way people grow food but also the ways they think about it. In the Western industrial system, abstract, rational, objective (masculine) knowledge about food and nutrition is privileged over experiential or applied knowledge. This scientific approach leads to reducing food to component parts like protein or fats. Then scientific nutritional guidelines quantify how much of these parts to eat in what proportion. This quantification has created a new reality by reducing food to a quantitative measurement (Hayes-Conroy and Hayes-Conroy 2013; Mudry 2009). Calories, for example, did not exist prior to the use of the calorimeter, and although no one can taste, see, touch, or smell a calorie, people know they exist because they can read the food label and count how many of them are in a serving. Even the notion of separating food into portions based on some specified amount (i.e., serving size based on ounces or cups) is an aspect of our mainstream nutrition knowledge. These quantitative measures become the only "real" way to know food, more accurate than "subjective" ways of knowing like taste or tradition because they can be identified and compared using numbers.

This kind of reductionism makes it easier for experts to standardize nutrition knowledge since numbers apply to populations, not particular people (Hayes-Conroy and Hayes-Conroy 2013; Mudry 2009; Scrinis 2013; Guthman 2011). Nutrition thus becomes a one-size-fits-all knowledge, even though individuals' nutritional needs, social context, and cultural traditions vary widely. The MyPlate guide to eating (figure 5.1) includes fruits/veggies, proteins, and carbohydrates in a particular combination and quantity designed to apply to all Americans, for example, regardless of their cultural backgrounds and/or social contexts.

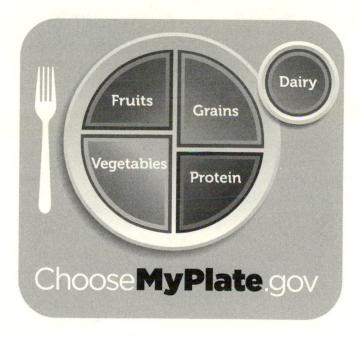

Figure 5.1.   USDA MyPlate.

G. Scrinis (2013) makes a similar argument, stating that nutrition science has reduced food to nutrients (such as vitamins, for instance), which are then used to make decisions about what and how much food to eat. He terms this ideology "nutritionalism," which he claims has been the dominant paradigm for nutrition science for the past century and served

as the foundation of dietary guidelines since the 1960s and food marketing since the 1980s. Nutrition science reduces food to nutrients and then
makes recommendations based on these scientific parts, regardless of how
the food fits into a healthy diet, traditional knowledges about food, and/
or individual tastes. Isolating individual nutrients also ignores interactions
that can occur between single nutrients within foods and in other food
combinations (Scrinis 2013).

The abstraction of food knowledge from social context makes it easier for
experts to attribute moral categories to food choices, distinctions that are
utilized in creating boundaries separating good and bad eaters. Race and
social class figure prominently in these distinctions. Early social reformers
like Ellen Richards, the founder of home economics in the United States,
worked to establish a standard American diet to bring healthier (and scientific) food practices to immigrants, thus elevating certain racial groups over
others through food choice (Biltekoff 2013). In another historical example,
nutritionists and government bureaucrats contrasted the better "American"
diet of meat and milk with the rice and vegetable diet of the Chinese and
determined that the Chinese diet produced inferior bodies. The following
statement from a U.S. Department of Agriculture spokesperson in 1928 ex-
emplifies the racial boundaries food knowledge can create: "Today, the Chinese is peaceful, sagacious, unprogressive, unenterprising, non-persevering;
his stature is poor, his physique bad, his mortality high" (quoted in DuPuis
2015, 89). This message inferred not just that certain foods affect growth
but that non-American (nonscientific) diets resulted in inferior citizens.

Obesity is a contemporary example of how health and nutrition are
standardized, reduced to numbers determined by experts, and used to
determine which bodies are worthy of society's approval. The body mass
index (BMI) is a ratio of weight to height, and as a statistical measurement,
it is used to divide the population of the United States into five categories:
underweight, normal, overweight, obese, and morbidly obese. This number,
devised as a shorthand for simple physical measurements, supposedly represents an individual's potential for health, as weight has been correlated
with a range of negative outcomes based on studies of populations. However, this measurement does not actually measure fat (adiposity); nor does
it provide a clinical assessment of health for specific individual bodies
(Guthman 2011). Studies find, for instance, that people with BMIs in the
overweight range may actually live longer than those with lower BMIs (Flegal et al. 2005; Campos et al. 2006). That the categories are actually socially
constructed and may not actually reflect reality was evident in 1998 when
the National Institutes of Health changed the BMI criteria and overnight 25
million "normal" Americans became "overweight" (Guthman 2011).

While it is difficult to dispute that an extreme excess of pounds can
lead to higher probabilities of some types of medical conditions for some

people, the medical establishment has used the BMI as the benchmark for determining which bodies are categorized as "fat." In effect, the BMI defines not only what types of bodies are "normal" and "not normal" from a medical standpoint but also what is socially desirable, what our bodies ought to be. As opposed to a more comprehensive measure of health that would determine more clearly whether individual bodies are really healthy, the BMI uses a simplistic set of measurements to determine whether individual bodies are really worthy or desirable. In other words, the terms "overweight" and "obese" are prescriptive rather than descriptive; they are socially constructed to sanction some bodies and reward others. Thin bodies are rewarded because they signal that the individual has exhibited self-control and willpower. By extension fat bodies are unhealthy, and the individual has failed and is an unworthy citizen (LeBesco 2004).

The neoliberal focus on individual responsibility turbo-charged the social tendency to blame individuals for weight gain. Medical and popular dieting advice during the 1990s and early 2000s concluded that losing weight was just a matter of decreasing calories, eating the right food, and increasing physical activity (Biltekoff 2013; Guthman 2011). Current research suggests that losing weight may not be within the individual's control once the weight has already been gained, making the social causes of weight gain even more important to explore. Fat studies scholars and proponents of "health at any size" point out that while there are negative health outcomes associated with being overweight, in fact stress, poverty, and marginalization might be stronger triggers for diseases such as diabetes than weight per se (Bacon and Aphramor 2011).

Obesity is not uniform across the population of the United States. On average, 38 percent of women are obese, compared to 34 percent of men. However, averages obscure differences in obesity rates among racial and ethnic categories and socioeconomic classes. White non-Hispanic women have much lower rates of obesity than African American and Hispanic women: 54.8 percent of non-Hispanic black women were obese in 2017, compared with 50.6 percent of Hispanic women, 38 percent of non-Hispanic white women, and 14.8 percent of non-Hispanic Asian women (Hales et al. 2017). Within each racial category, rates of obesity for women rise with levels of poverty. For men, with the exception of Asian men, rates of obesity were roughly the same across racial categories, although higher obesity rates occur at higher income levels for African American and Hispanic men (Ogden et al. 2010) (see figure 5.2).

American society stigmatizes fat bodies. Overweight and obese individuals experience discrimination in nearly every aspect of their lives (Sobal 2008). Women in particular report discrimination at lower weights then men. In a national survey of middle-aged Americans, men did not report significant discrimination until a BMI of thirty-five or higher, whereas

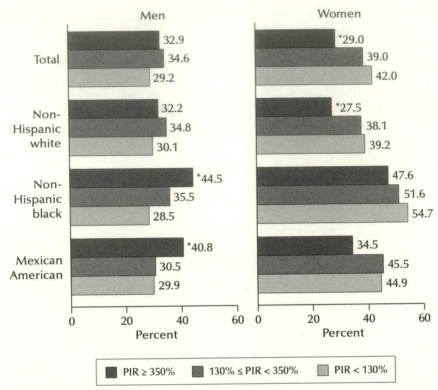

Figure 5.2. Prevalence of obesity by sex and income levels, 2005–2008 (CDC/NCHS, National Health and Nutrition Examination Survey, 2005–2008, in Ogden et al. 2010).
* Significant trend
Note: PIR is poverty income ratio. Persons of other races and ethnicities are included in the total.

women experienced a notable increase in weight/height discrimination risk at a BMI level of twenty-seven (Puhl, Andreyeva, and Brownell 2008). Women reported discrimination in hiring practices and in interpersonal relationships, lower lifetime earnings, and lower rates of marriage (Conley and Glauber 2007; Gortmaker et al. 1993). Being "overweight" can also lead to an increased rate of unnecessary medical interventions, such as surgery and pharmaceuticals, even when the person is healthy. Due to physicians' and other health professionals' biased and negative attitudes toward overweight people, some overweight people delay preventative medical care such as Pap smears and cancer screenings (Paquette and Raine 2004). The lack of appropriately sized medical equipment may also prevent individuals from receiving proper medical care.

Feminists argue that food nutrition and knowledge are really about power. Alison and Jessica Hayes-Conroy suggest that a process of "dietary decolonization" is necessary to relocalize food systems and recenter food practices pushed aside by industrial food knowledge. Democratic nutrition knowledge construction is necessary, and rather than allowing experts to retain the authority over food knowledge, communities should produce knowledge about healthy food out of their histories, traditions, and experiences. This process would also decenter whiteness, a central aspect of industrial food knowledge, "by realizing that *the very impulse or desire to engage* in food activism might be, quite expressly, *not* white" (Hayes-Conroy and Hayes-Conroy 2013, 181; italics in original). Scientists, instead of taking an objective, supposedly neutral stance, would engage with political economic and social critiques to create a more socially embedded nutrition knowledge.

CONCLUSION

Gender norms shape every aspect of the food system, right down to the choice of what foods to put on one's plate. Normative models of masculinity and femininity prescribe certain food categories for certain people. Men are expected to consume heavy, protein-dense foods in a dietary holdover from the times when heavy physical labor was standard; to eat otherwise is to risk having one's masculinity questioned or denigrated. Women's eating, on the other hand, is characterized by what is not consumed. "Light" foods, such as salad and fruits, keep women's bodies small and their femininity intact. These gendered standards are situational, however: different cultures and social classes have their own standards for masculine and feminine eating. One example is "foodie" culture, in which upper-class men can gain social capital from cooking and from eating food that is often light, expensive, and served in small portions.

These eating practices serve as the physical manifestation of cultural standards, with the body serving as a marker of successfully performed gender. Women's bodies are policed more strictly, both through media representations and through interpersonal interactions. The unattainably thin bodies prevalent in advertising and other media are taking a toll on the mental health of women from an early age, with girls expressing an interest in dieting at younger and younger ages. Although the most common image of an eating disorder may be an overly thin white girl, eating disorders impact members of all groups, including men and women of all racial and class backgrounds.

Modern diet culture, which contributes to the prevalence of eating disorders in both men and women, is rooted in an ideal of personal responsibility. In this mode of thinking, individual consumers are entirely responsible for their own food choices. To be overweight, then, is seen as a personal and moral failure. Of course, this school of thought completely overlooks the systems of power that impact individual's food choices. From overproducing cheaper vegetables with lower nutrient content to heavily marketing sugary and fatty processed foods, corporate players in the food system have an effect on individual food choice.

Another way individual food behavior is influenced by corporations is through the proliferation of "nutritionalism," a way of understanding food that privileges scientific over socially transmitted knowledge. This method reduces food to its component parts, even though these component parts (such as the calorie, which was unknown before the invention of the calorimeter) are invisible to consumers. This scientific focus led to the creation of the BMI, which sorts people into weight categories despite being an inaccurate measure of actual health. As a result, some groups are pushing for a return to more traditional and socially grounded ways of knowing about food and eating.

NOTES

1. One of the most egregious examples of photoshopping was a 2009 advertisement for Ralph Lauren in which Filippa Hamilton's waist was smaller than her head.

2. In a perverse way, then, capitalists and the associated corporations they own benefit from the unhealthy consequences of a corporate agrifood system by profiting from providing services to people whose bodies have been negatively impacted by industrial food. Our food system is very likely to contribute to unhealthy eating practices through agribusiness models that support commodity food production, which produces some foods in excess (corn and soybeans, for example) but not enough healthy foods. In this system, manufacturing companies produce foods high in fat, sugar, and salt in order to capture value-added profits, and the retail distribution system shunts healthy food-fruits, vegetables, and choice into middle-class and often white neighborhoods (discussed in chapters 2 and 3 of this book). In fact, maintaining the focus on individual behaviors as the cause of increasing weight keeps us from questioning the contribution of the industrial food system to these problems (Gottlieb and Joshi 2010; Guthman 2011; Julier 2013).

3. Thanks to a reviewer for this suggestion.

CHAPTER 6

Conclusion

Examining the food system as a whole reveals gendered patterns in the division of labor and power in growing, buying, cooking, and eating food in Western society. In the realms of growing, production, and distribution, privileged white men are more likely to own and manage corporations, restaurants, and supermarkets and thus to make important business and political decisions about what foods are produced, distributed, and marketed. Men comprise 72 percent of CEOs of food companies and comprise 85 percent of the membership on the corporate boards of food companies (Yen Liu and Apollan 2010). Men are more likely to be the politicians who make policies and laws to regulate the food system; in the United States, 80 percent of federal legislators and 75 percent of state legislators are men. Men are more likely to be agricultural scientists who develop new farming technologies. Even the farmers and ranchers who grow our food (in the Global North) and the chefs at celebrity and elite restaurants are men. The people in these positions wield considerable power over food and agricultural policy, effectively setting the rules for what food is produced, how it is distributed, and where in the system resources are allocated.

Not only are more men in positions of power in the food system, but these positions are also associated with particular forms of masculinity. In business, leaders are assumed to be risk takers, aggressive, determined, and strong (Pini 2005). The traits associated with farming—or an agrarian masculinity—are endurance, physical strength, knowledge of machines, and independence. The elite professional chef is competitive and does not show emotion in the face of intense pressure. For women, the association between masculinity and business or farming makes it more difficult to enter these professions and/or rise to leadership positions. For men, these forms of masculinity can also lead to negative consequences; farmers who are men, for example, have high rates of suicide, and chefs who are men experience high levels of substance abuse.

Not all men experience the same levels of privilege in this system. Men of color are far less likely to be managers or owners and more likely to work in low-paying positions on the farm or in the back of restaurants as cooks and dishwashers (Jayaraman 2013; Sachs et al. 2014). African American men are far less likely to be farmers due to land appropriation by whites under Jim Crow in the U.S. South and discrimination by the U.S. Department of Agriculture, as well as their disproportionate incarceration rate in the U.S. criminal justice system. North American farmers exploit the work of immigrant men, often Hispanic, who as farmworkers are hired to pick and harvest crops not amenable to mechanization, such as produce and fruits, and are exposed to pesticides and other toxic chemicals in the process.

Occupational segregation disadvantages women across the production and distribution system. Women are more likely than men to be employed in service jobs in retail and restaurants—for instance, as cashiers or low-level managers in supermarkets or as servers at family-owned or fast-food restaurants. These jobs pay low wages, offer few opportunities for advancement, lack benefits such as sick leave or retirement, and require nonstandard working hours, which make balancing work and family difficult. Women in the West are entering farming as principal operators at higher rates than in the past, but their farms tend to be smaller, less mechanized, and less profitable than men's. Farmworkers who are women make up a smaller percentage of the total number of farmworkers but work in some of the lowest-paying and lowest-status jobs such as pickers and sorters. Again, not all women experience the same level of privilege in this system. White women are more likely to be working as farmers or managers or even chefs. Women of color and women without citizenship status are more likely to be working in the fields or in low-level service jobs.

However, all women confront the threat of violence across the food system. Men, as employers, coworkers, and customers, sexually harass and assault women in fields, in restaurants, and in grocery stores, practices that are symptomatic of the disproportionate power men wield in the food system. Food is even a trigger for domestic violence in the home. As more women speak out about their experiences with abuse and harassment, this may change; however, workers with undocumented status or in precarious nonunionized positions may not be able to bring allegations forward due to the threat of deportation or job loss.

Globally, women are still responsible for household foodwork. In the United States and Canada, where at least half of adult women work for wages, women still cook and shop twice as much as men on average. Not only does the routine work of feeding people in households still fall on women, but the successful accomplishment of femininity is predicated on this labor. To be a good mother or spouse entails feeding others appropriately. Whereas once the accomplishment of this feeding standard meant cooking a meal of meat and starches, women are now responsible for the health and nutrition of the food they are serving the family. This responsibility is magnified by discourses such as ethical consumption, intensive mothering, and the (neoliberal) personal responsibility for health, which positions women and mothers as the primary household food- and careworker.

Women's food labor not only benefits households but also knits together different parts of the food system. Without women's work in grocery shopping, for example, the goods produced at one end of the food system would not make it into household pantries. Shoppers' unpaid labor coordinates the needs and tastes of family and household members with the business practices of supermarkets, grocery stores, and even farmers' markets and thus completes the distribution cycle. This work leads to less leisure time for women and work-family conflicts that must be resolved. Critically, however, the shopper and the cook are at the end of the decision-making process about what food we will grow, what products will be on the grocery store shelves, what kind of stores are available, and even how these parts of the food chain are coordinated.

Men in the Global North are doing more cooking and shopping than in past generations, and some are even cooking and shopping regularly. However, their identities as men or fathers are not bound to their work in the kitchen; they do not have to regularly feed others to accomplish masculinity. In fact, a traditional culinary masculinity (Szabo 2014) entails food exploration, performance, conquest, or not cooking at all, but it is in no way predicated on making meals for others routinely as is a traditional culinary or food femininity.

Even the seemingly individual act of eating is gendered. In Western societies, "manly" eating is associated with heavy foods such as meat, fat, and alcohol, and society allows men to eat higher quantities and with more gusto without judgment. Some men, if their social class is high enough, can deviate and eat more feminine foods such as vegetables and fruit. Stereotypical masculine eating can have negative individual health and environmental consequences. Men live, on average, five years less than women (at least in the United States). This difference can be attributed to higher rates of heart disease, which is associated with a diet heavy in saturated fat. A masculine food identity tied to autonomy and independence may also prevent men from taking health advice or eating in more "feminine" ways, such as ingesting fewer calories and less meat or more fruits and vegetables even after illness.

The association between meat and masculinity has global significance, as meat production, processing, and distribution are central to the global food system (Gouveia and Juska 2002). Producing meat requires huge amounts of pesticides, fertilizer, fuel, feed, and water and has the effect of releasing greenhouse gases, creating manure, and putting a range of toxic chemicals into our air and water. In fact, food researchers suggest that one of the most sustainable changes an individual could make would be to switch to a vegetarian diet. As more people across the world achieve middle-class status and are able to afford meat protein, this association between meat, masculinity, and class will have potentially disastrous environmental consequences and may impede progress toward developing more sustainable diets.

Feminine eating is light and insubstantial and entails vegetables, salads, and sweets. Expectations for a particular body type are also associated with food femininities. A majority of women in most Western countries are on diets, and this behavior starts for many when they are girls. However, Kate Cairns and Josee Johnston (2015) find that women are not supposed to go to extremes and, while still being ultimately concerned with these issues, must exhibit a balance in eating/dieting and caregiving. Body and eating expectations are also connected to a white middle-class norm of thin and fit bodies. This "tyranny of slenderness" (Chernin 1981) fosters an antagonistic relationship between women and food and for some can lead to eating disorders. Businesses that provide weight-loss programs, diet pills, and even medical procedures profit from this unhealthy relationship between food and society's expectations for women's bodies. The irony is that, in Western cultures at least, women are supposed to deny themselves food that industrial agriculture produces in excess as a normal part of its operating procedure. Not only are women's eating patterns scrutinized, but society stigmatizes and discriminates against fat bodies. This discrimination disproportionately affects poor individuals and women of color, who are more likely to be overweight and obese as a result of the detrimental effects of a food system that produces way too much cheap, unhealthy food. Men's bodies are increasingly pulled into this capitalist orbit, as products and diets for men's bodies have also proliferated in recent years.

These patterns I've identified through a review of food scholarship are predicated on conceptual dichotomies that prioritize production over reproduction, the market over the household, and, ultimately, masculinity over femininity. The power of a gendered (and intersectional) lens is the ability to analyze the food system across conceptual boundaries—public/private, market/household—to show that the outcome of a gendered capitalist system, including segregated occupations, a male-dominated political-economic power structure, the devaluation of unpaid food labor, and expectations for food femininities and masculinities, privilege some people and some kinds of foodwork over others *systematically*. Let me give an example: Farmers and parents both feed people, one indirectly by growing food, the other directly by purchasing and cooking food. However, the U.S. government redistributes money from taxes in ways that privilege male workers over female provisioners. Money earmarked for workers who own land to grow food—farmers, who are overwhelmingly male—is considered a "subsidy." (Remember that most of the $211 billion in farm subsidies the government paid between 1995 and 2009 went to the biggest farms growing wheat, corn, and soybeans and ranches producing meat, so not all farmers benefit in similar ways.) But when the government gives tax dollars to families to support food purchases, it is considered "welfare." The government spent $74.1 billion in 2014 on the Supplemental Nutrition Assistance Program (SNAP; formerly known as food stamps) and helped roughly 46.5 million Americans by providing an average of $125.35 per person per month to buy food (Dean and Rosenbaum 2013). These categories and the government's subsequent allocation of benefits between them are based on dichotomies of public/private and paid/unpaid work. In essence, the government gives subsidies to "worthy" workers who produce something for the economy (i.e., farmers), while it doles out welfare to the undeserving nonworker or food provisioner. The gendered distinction between giving waged workers "subsidies" and unpaid provisioners "welfare" clearly structures these policies.

However, in reality, many SNAP recipients are working. Policy researchers at the Center on Budget and Policy Priorities (CBPP) calculated in 2012 that nearly 75 percent of adults who participated in SNAP in an average month had worked either that month or within a year of that month (Keith-Jennings and Chaudhry 2018). As one of the main criteria for SNAP benefits is income at or below poverty level (about $20,400 for a family of three in 2016), many low-wage food workers qualify. In fact, workers in service occupations such as cooks, servers, and cashiers use SNAP more than members of any other occupation (CBPP 2017). Putting food on the table is much more difficult for women when employers pay them less than men (and for women of color this means less than white women too), they face harassment at work for their gender and/or sexuality, and there is little public support for private foodwork. Precisely this combination of devalued household labor in the public sphere (through unequal resource distribution) and devalued women's labor in the market (by employers and through a gendered division of labor) disadvantages women in both the public and the private realms.

Even further, 70 percent of SNAP households include children, and of those households, 47 percent are headed by single mothers. Now, imagine your gendered identity is intimately tied to feeding people, but you are not able to provide food for your family. You may have to make the horrible decision about which child to feed or whether to feed your children and not eat yourself. What kind of damage does this do to individual bodies, to individual subjectivities? How is true food security possible when the burden of provisioning is left to households without resources?

FUTURE RESEARCH AND ACTIVISM

I acknowledge that the attention I devote to gender as a key aspect of a capitalist food system may not capture all experiences or perspectives. Studies on the impact of sexuality on food production and distribution, for example, were difficult to find, and more research is certainly warranted to fill in these missing pieces. Nor does my analysis include all aspects of the food system. Food disposal and waste is a growing field of scholarship that I had to overlook due to space constraints. As food scholars begin to devote more attention to food waste, it will be increasingly necessary to look at the gendered and raced aspects of that process. I also chose to examine scholarship on the food system from the vantage of the United States and other Western countries and acknowledge that this research is not complete without more study of global systems.

In general, though, a gendered lens suggests the necessity for scholars and activists to explore the food system from the perspective of those most marginalized, including women, people of color, children, and people in the Global South, and to make explicit the connections between the different domains of the food system. It also suggests that those with the most responsibility for feeding others should play a significant role in the decision-making process. Penny Van Esterik (1999) equates women's rights with food security and argues,

> Women are *most likely* to be responsible for feeding their families on a daily basis, and *least likely* to be involved in shaping the policies that determine the food system they must access. The movement of food at the international, national, and even regional level is almost invariably male controlled; but the mediators of food at the individual, household, and community level are usually women. Hunger is experienced not by states but by individuals. It is thus critical that women's role in alleviating hunger be more fully recognized and integrated into policy planning. Policies must include consideration of such labor intensive practices as breastfeeding infants, feeding toddlers, supervising child feeding, coaxing sick and elderly to eat, as well as producing, processing, preparing, marketing, and trading food. (231)

Patricia Allen (2008) reminds us that "since the agrifood system is socially organized, problems are the product of social choices, embodied in traditions, institutions, and legal and economic structures" (160). If this is true, then problems with the food system that result from the systems of inequality I've identified in this book can be dismantled by changing traditions and institutions. To start, we need more representation at the tables of power by those whose lives are negatively impacted by current political economic decisions. This is not inconceivable. In Europe, for example, countries such as Iceland, Norway, Germany, and France have instituted quotas for the number of women on corporate boards, a policy that has doubled women's participation in the business realm in a short amount of time. Of course, this doesn't necessarily equate to changes in economic or business policy, but it broadens the background of individuals in these governing bodies, leading to a higher likelihood of policies that benefit marginalized members of society.

Greater participation of men in caregiving will also be necessary in order to undercut the inequality inherent in the food system. A more equal distribution of provisioning work in the household will require men to give up some time and freedom in order for women to regain it, while a greater focus on caring for others in the workplace requires more commitment from its leaders. Both of these changes involve altering expectations for masculinity and femininity. Recent political wins by women in the United States offer new images and associations between femininity and leadership, for example, and it is not inconceivable that societies can rework masculinity to prioritize caring and caregiving over domination. Scholarship suggests that men who do a good portion of the routine foodwork in the household tend to cook in ways more like women, such as to show love, care for others, and so forth (Szabo 2014).

Interrogating the causes and acting to redress gender and other inequalities in the food system may also lead to greater environmental sustainability. If the people who actually feed others, whether it be farmers, cooks, or parents—as members of their local communities—were able to make the decisions about how and what food to grow, how that food should be distributed, and who is entitled to eat the food, perhaps pressure to use synthetic inputs or to plant in monocultures or to produce processed food would diminish. La Via Campesina is one possible model of connecting community food sovereignty and social equality with environmental sustainability. This organization brings together small and medium-size farmers, landless people, rural women and youth, indigenous people, migrants, and agricultural workers from around the world in order to challenge the industrial food system that keeps so many hungry and landless with new ways of organizing and growing. Women's inclusion in leadership is one of the organization's explicit goals and in fact La Via Campesina champions indigenous and local knowledges in order to grow and distribute food sustainably and equitably. Ultimately, sustainability, equity, and justice should be the goal of any food system.

References

Aarseth, Helene and Bente Marianne Olsen. 2008. "Food and Masculinity in Dual-Career Couples." *Journal of Gender Studies* 17(4): 277–287.

Abarca, Meredith. 2006. *Voices in the Kitchen: Views of Food and the World from Working-Class Mexican and Mexican-American Women*. College Station: Texas A&M University Press.

Acker, Joan. 2006. *Class Questions, Feminist Answers*. Lanham, MD: Rowman & Littlefield.

Adams, C. J. 1990. *The Sexual Politics of Meat: A Feminist-Vegetarian Critical Theory*. 20th century ed. New York: Continuum Publishing Company.

Adler, Thomas A. 1981. "Making Pancakes on Sunday: The Male Cook in Family Tradition." *Western Folklore* 40(1): 45–54.

Alkon, Alison Hope. 2014. "Food Justice and the Challenge to Neoliberalism." *Gastronomica: The Journal of Critical Food Studies* 14(2): 27–40.

Alkon, Alison Hope and Julian Agyeman, eds. 2011. *Cultivating Food Justice: Race, Class, and Sustainability*. Cambridge, MA: MIT Press.

Alkon, Alison Hope and Julie Guthman. 2017. *The New Food Activism: Opposition, Cooperation, and Collective Action*. Berkeley: University of California Press.

Alkon, Alison Hope and Christie Grace McCullen. 2011. "Whiteness and Farmers Markets: Performances, Perpetuations . . . Contestations?" *Antipode* 43(4): 937–959.

Allen, Patricia. 2004. *Together at the Table: Sustainability and Sustenance in the American Agrifood System*. University Park: Pennsylvania State University Press.

———. 2008. "Mining for Justice in the Food System: Perceptions, Practices, and Possibilities." *Agriculture and Human Values* 25: 157–161.

Allen, P. and C. Sachs. 2007. "Women and Food Chains: The Gendered Politics of Food." *International Journal of Sociology of Food and Agriculture* 15(1): 1–23.

Allison, Anne. 2013 [1999]. "Japanese Mothers and Obentos: The Lunch-Box as Ideological State Apparatus." In *Food and Culture: A Reader*, edited by Carole Counihan and Penny Van Esterik, 154–172. New York: Routledge.

Anderson, Margo. 1994. "(Only) White Men Have Class: Reflections on Early 19th Century Occupational Classification Systems." *Work and Occupations* 21(1): 5–32.

Association of Farmworker Opportunity Programs (AFOP). 2012. "The Fields: The Hidden Faces of Farmworker Women." AFOP. http://afop.org/wp-content/up loads/2010/07/The-Fields-PDF-2.13-version.pdf.

Australian Bureau of Statistics. 2009. "Trends in Household Work." *Australian Social Trends*. March. Accessed June 5, 2015. http://www.abs.gov.au/ausstats/abs@.nsf/ Lookup/4102.0Main+Features40March%202009.

Avakian, A. V. 2005. *Through the Kitchen Window: Women Explore the Intimate Meanings of Food and Cooking*. 2nd ed. New York: Berg.

Avakian, A. V. and B. Haber. 2005. "Feminist Food Studies: A Brief History." In *From Betty Crocker to Feminist Food Studies: Critical Perspectives on Women and Food*, edited by A. Avakian and B. Haber, 1–28. Boston: University of Massachusetts Press.

Bacon, Linda and Lucy Aphramor. 2011. "Weight Science: Evaluating the Evidence for a Paradigm Shift." *Nutrition Journal* 10(9): 1–13.

Barbercheck, Mary, Katherine Brasier, Nancy Ellen Kiernan, Carolyn Sachs, Amy Trauger, and Jill Findeis. 2009. "Meeting the Extension Needs of Women Farmers: A Perspective from Pennsylvania." *Journal of Extension* 47(3).

Barndt, Deborah. 2008. *Tangled Routes: Women, Work and Globalization on the Tomato Trail*. 2nd ed. Lanham, MD: Rowman & Littlefield Publishers.

Barrientos, Stephanie, Andrienetta Kritzinger, Maggie Opondo, and Sally Smith. 2005. "Gender, Work and Vulnerability in African Horticulture." *IDS Bulletin* 36(2): 74–79.

Bartky, Sandra Lee. 1990. *Femininity and Domination: Studies in the Phenomenology of Oppression*. New York: Routledge.

Basow, Susan A. and Diane Kobrynowicz. 1993. "What Is She Eating? The Effects of Meal Size on Impressions of a Female Eater." *Sex Roles* 28(5–6): 335–344.

Bauer, Mary and Monica Ramirez. 2010. "Injustice on Our Plates: Immigrant Women in the U.S. Food Industry." Montgomery: Southern Poverty Law Center.

Beach, Sarah. 2013. "'Tractorettes' or Partners? Farmers' Views on Women in Kansas Farming Households." *Rural Sociology* 78(2): 210–228.

Beagan, Brenda, Gwen E. Chapman, Andrea D'Sylva, and B. Raewyn Bassett. 2008. "'It's Just Easier for Me to Do It': Rationalizing the Family Division of Foodwork." *Sociology* 42(4): 653–671.

Beagan, Brenda L. and Gwen E. Chapman. 2012. "Meanings of Food, Eating and Health Among African Nova Scotians: 'Certain Things Aren't Meant for Black Folk.'" *Ethnicity & Health* 17(5): 513–529.

Beardsworth, A. and T. Keil. 1997. *Sociology on the Menu: An Invitation to the Study of Food and Society*. London: Routledge.

Beauboeuf-Lefontant, Tamara. 2009. *Behind the Mask of the Strong Black Woman: Voice and the Embodiment of a Costly Performance*. Philadelphia: Temple University Press.

Bell, David and Gill Valentine. 1997. *Consuming Geographies: We Are Where We Eat*. London and New York: Routledge.

Bently, Amy. 2004. "The Other Atkins Revolution: Atkins and the Shifting Culture of Dieting." *Gastronomica* 4(3): 34–45.

Beoku-Betts, Josephine A. 1995. "We Got Our Way of Cooking Things: Women, Food, and Preservation of Cultural Identity Among the Gullah." *Gender and Society* 9(5): 535–555.

Beren, S. E., H. A. Hayden, D. E. Wilfley, and C. M. Grilo. 1996. "The Influence of Sexual Orientation on Body Dissatisfaction in Adult Men and Women." *International Journal of Eating Disorders* 20: 135–141.

Beus, Curtis and Riley Dunlap. 1990. "Conventional vs. Alternative Agriculture: The Paradigmatic Roots of the Debate." *Rural Sociology* 55(4): 590–616.

Bianchi, Suzanne M., Melissa A. Milkie, Liana C. Sayer, and John P. Robinson. 2000. "Is Anyone Doing the Housework? Trends in the Gender Division of Household Labor?" *Social Forces* 79(1): 191–228.

Biltekoff, Charlotte. 2013. *Eating Right in America: The Cultural Politics of Food and Health*. Durham, NC: Duke University Press.

BLS (U.S. Bureau of Labor Statistics). 2014a. "Employment and Wages for the Highest and Lowest Paying Occupations." Occupational Employment Statistics. May. Accessed March 9, 2015. http://www.bls.gov/oes/2014/may/high_low_paying.htm.

———. 2014b. "Women in the Labor Force: A Databook." BLS. Accessed December 2014. https://www.bls.gov/cps/wlf-databook-2013.pdf.

———. 2015a. "American Time Use Survey: 2014 Results." BLS. Accessed April 29, 2016. http://www.bls.gov/news.release/pdf/atus.pdf.

———. 2015b. "Employment, Hours, and Earnings from Current Employment Statistics." BLS. August. Accessed April 20, 2017. www.bls.gov/ces.

———. 2016a. "National Census of Fatal Occupational Injuries in 2016." BLS. Accessed June 2016. https://www.bls.gov/news.release/pdf/cfoi.pdf.

———. 2016b. "Highlights of Women's Earnings in 2016." BLS. Accessed November 11, 2018. https://www.bls.gov/opub/reports/womens-earnings/2016/home.htm.

———. 2017a. "Occupational Employment and Wages, May 2017 35-3021 Combined Food Preparation and Serving Workers, Including Fast Food." BLS. Accessed June 1, 2017. https://www.bls.gov/oes/current/oes353021.htm.

———. 2017b. "Occupational Outlook Handbook, Agricultural and Food Scientists." BLS. Accessed January 4, 2017. https://www.bls.gov/ooh/life-physical-and-social-science/agricultural-and-food-scientists.htm.

———. 2017c. "Occupational Outlook Handbook, Dietitians and Nutritionists." BLS. Accessed January 4, 2017. https://www.bls.gov/ooh/healthcare/dietitians-and-nutritionists.htm.

Boone-Heinonen, J., P. Gordon-Larsen, C. I. Kiefe, J. M. Shikany, C. E. Lewis, and B. M. Popkin. 2011. "Fast Food Restaurants and Food Stores: Longitudinal Associations with Diet in Young to Middle-Aged Adults: The CARDIA Study." *Archives of Internal Medicine* 171(13): 1162–1170.

Bordo, Susan. 1993. *Unbearable Weight: Feminism, Western Culture, and the Body*. Berkeley: University of California Press.

———. 2013. "Not Just 'a White Girl's Thing': The Changing Face of Food and Body Image Problems." In *Food and Culture: A Reader*, edited by Carole Counihan and Penny Van Esterik, 265–275. New York: Routledge.

Bose, Christine E. 1984. "Household Resources and U.S. Women's Work: Factors Affecting Gainful Employment at the Turn of the Century." *American Sociological Review* 49: 474–490.

Boserup, E. 1970. *Woman's Role in Economic Development*. New York: St. Martin's Press.

Bouchard, Maryse F., Jonathan Chevrier, Kim G. Harley, Katherine Kogut, Michelle Vedar, Norma Calderon, Celina Trujillo, Caroline Johnson, Asa Bradman, Dana Boyd Barr, and Brenda Eskenazi1. 2011. "Prenatal Exposure to Organophosphate Pesticides and IQ in 7-Year-Old Children." *Environmental Health Perspectives* 119(8): 1190–1195.

Bourdieu, Pierre. 1984. *Distinction: A Social Critique of the Judgement of Taste*. Cambridge, MA: Harvard University Press.

Bove, Caron F. and Jeffery Sobal. 2006. "Foodwork in Newly Married Couples." *Food, Culture and Society* 9(1): 70–89.

Bowen, Sarah, Sinikka Elliott, and Joslyn Brenton. 2014. "The Joy of Cooking?" *Contexts* 13: 20–25.

Bowlby, Rachael. 1997. "Supermarket Futures." In *The Shopping Experience*, edited by Pasi Falk and Colin Campbell, 92–110. London: Sage.

Brandth, Berit. 1995. "Rural Masculinity in Transition: Gender Images in Tractor Advertisements." *Journal of Rural Studies* 11(2): 123–133.

——. 2002. "Gender Identity in European Family Farming: A Literature Review." *Sociologia Ruralis* 42: 181–200.

——. 2006. "Agricultural Body-Building: Incorporations of Gender, Body and Work." *Journal of Rural Studies* 22: 17–27.

Brandth, Berit and M. S. Haugen. 1998. "Breaking into a Masculine Discourse: Women and Farm Forestry." *Sociologia Ruralis* 38(3): 427–442.

——. 2000. "From Lumberjack to Business Manager: Masculinity in the Norwegian Forestry Press."*Journal of Rural Studies* 16(3): 343–355.

Bray, G., S. J. Nielsen, and B. M. Popkin. 2004. "Consumption of High-Fructose Corn Syrup in Beverages May Play a Role in the Epidemic of Obesity." *American Journal of Clinical Nutrition* 79(4): 537–543.

Breen, R. and L. P. Cooke. 2005. "The Persistence of the Gendered Division of Labor." *European Sociological Review* 21: 43–57.

Brenton, Joslyn. 2017. "The Limits of Intensive Feeding: Maternal Foodwork at the Intersections of Race, Class, and Gender." *Sociology of Health & Illness* 39 (6): 863–877.

Brines, J. 1994. "Economic Dependency, Gender, and the Division-of-Labor at Home." *American Journal of Sociology* 100: 652–688.

Bruce, Analena and Rebecca L. Som Castellano. 2017. "Labor and Alternative Food Networks: Challenges for Farmers and Consumers." *Renewable Agriculture and Food Systems* 32(5): 403–416.

Buckingham, S. 2005. "Women (Re)construct the Plot: The Regen(d)eration of Urban Food Growing." *Area* 37(2): 171–179.

Budig, Michelle J. and Paula England. 2001. "The Wage Penalty for Motherhood." *American Sociological Review* 66(2): 204–225.

Buerkle, C. W. 2012. "Metrosexuality Can Stuff It: Beef Consumption as (Heteromasculine) Fortification." In *Taking Food Public: Redefining Foodways in a Changing World*, edited by P. Williams-Forson and C. Counihan, 251–264. New York: Routledge.

Burch, D. and G. Lawrence. 2007. "Supermarket Own-Brands, New Foods and the Reconfiguration of Agri-food Supply Chains." In *Supermarkets and Agri-food Supply Chains*, edited by D. Burch and G. Lawrence, 100–128. London: Edward Elgar.

Busch, Lawrence and William B. Lacy. 1983. *Science, Agriculture, and the Politics of Research*. Boulder: CO: Westview Press.

Buttel, F. and J. Goldberger. 2002. "Gender and Agricultural Science: Evidence from Two Surveys of Land-Grant Scientists." *Rural Sociology* 67(1): 24–43.

Cairns, Kate and Josee Johnston. 2015. *Food and Femininity*. London: Bloomsbury.

Cairns, Kate, Josee Johnston, and Shyon Baumann. 2010. "Caring About Food: Doing Gender in the Foodie Kitchen." *Gender and Society* 24(5): 591–615.

Cairns, Kate, Josee Johnston, and Norah Mackendrick. 2013. "Feeding the 'Organic Child': Mothering Through Ethical Consumption." *Journal of Consumer Culture* 13(2): 97–118.

Campos, P., A. Saguy, P. Ernsberger, E. Oliver, and G. Gaesser. 2006. "The Epidemiology of Overweight and Obesity: Public Health Crisis or Moral Panic?" *International Journal of Epidemiology* 35: 55–60. https://doi.org/10.1093/ije/dyi254.

Campos, Paul. 2004. *The Obesity Myth: Why America's Obsession with Weight Is Hazardous to Your Health*. New York: Gothom.

Carney, Megan. 2015. *The Unending Hunger*. Berkeley: University of California Press.

Carolan, Michael. 2012. *The Sociology of Food and Agriculture*. London: Routledge.

Carr, Edward R. 2008. "Men's Crops and Women's Crops: The Importance of Gender to the Understanding of Agricultural and Development Outcomes in Ghana's Central Region." *World Development* 36(5): 900–915.

Carrington, Christopher. 1999. *No Place like Home: Relationships and Family Life Among Lesbians and Gay Men*. Chicago: University of Chicago Press.

Center for Popular Democracy. 2016. "Data Brief: Retail Jobs Today." Accessed June 15, 2015. https://populardemocracy.org/sites/default/files/RetailJobsToday1.pdf.

Center on Budget and Policy Priorities (CBPP). 2017. "Policy Basics: Introduction to the Supplemental Nutrition Assistance Program (SNAP)." CBPP. Accessed August 9, 2017. https://www.cbpp.org/research/policy-basics-introduction-to-the-supple mental-nutrition-assistance-program-snap.

Charles, N. and M. Kerr. 1988. *Women, Food and Families*. Manchester, UK: Manchester University Press.

"Chefs and Head Cooks." N.d. Data USA. Accessed December 15, 2017. https://datausa.io/profile/soc/351011/#demographics.

Chernin, Kim. 1981. *The Obsession: Reflections on the Tyranny of Slenderness*. New York: Harper & Row.

Chiappe, Marta and Cornelia Butler Flora. 1998. "Gendered Elements of the Alternative Agriculture Paradigm." *Rural Sociology* 63(3): 372–393.

Collins, Jane. 1993. "Transnational Labor Process and Gender Relations: Women in Fruit and Vegetable Production in Chili, Brazil, and Mexico." *Journal of Latin American Anthropology* 1(1): 78–99.

———. 1995. "Gender and Cheap Labour in Agriculture." In *Food and Agrarian Orders in the World Economy*, edited by R. McMichael, 217–232. Westport, CT: Greenwood Press.

Conley, D. and R. Glauber. 2007. "Gender, Body Mass and Socioeconomic Status: New Evidence from the PSID." *Advances in Health Economics and Health Services Research* 17: 253–275.

Connell, R. W. 2005. *Masculinities*. 2nd ed. Oakland: University of California Press.

Connell, R. W. and J. W. Messerschmidt. 2005. "Hegemonic Masculinity: Rethinking the Concept." *Gender and Society* 19(6): 829–859.

Cook, Daniel. 2009. "Semantic Provisioning of Children's Food: Commerce, Care and Maternal Practice." *Childhood* 16(3): 317–334.

Cooke, L. J. and J. Wardle. 2005. "Age and Gender Differences in Children's Food Preferences." *British Journal of Nutrition* 93(5): 741–746.

Correll, Shelley J., Stephen Benard, and In Paik. 2007. "Getting a Job: Is There a Motherhood Penalty?" *American Journal of Sociology* 112(5): 1297–1339.

Counihan, Carole. 1999. *The Anthropology of Food and Body: Gender, Meaning and Power*. New York: Routledge.

———. 2005. "The Border as Barrier and Bridge: Food, Gender and Ethnicity in the San Luis Valley of Colorado." In *From Betty Crocker to Feminist Food Studies: Critical Perspectives on Women and Food*, edited by A. V. Arvakian and B. Haber, 200–217. Boston: University of Massachusetts Press.

———. 2012. "Gendering Food." In *The Oxford Handbook of Food History*, edited by Jeffery M. Pilcher, 99–116. Oxford: Oxford University Press.

Courtenay, William. 2000. "Constructions of Masculinity and Their Influence on Men's Well-Being: A Theory of Gender and Health." *Social Science and Medicine* 50: 1385–1401.

Coxon, T. 1983. "Men in the Kitchen: Notes from a Cookery Class." In *The Sociology of Food and Eating*, edited by A. Murcott, 172–177. Aldershot, UK: Gower Publishing.

Crawford, R. 1980. "Healthism and the Medicalization of Everyday Life." *International Journal of Health Services* 10(3): 365–388.

Crittenden, Ann. 2001. *The Price of Motherhood: Why the Most Important Job in the World Is Still the Least Valued*. New York: Metropolitan Books.

Daniels, Sarah and Ignace Glorieux. 2017. "Cooking Up Manliness: A Practice-Based Approach to Men's At-Home Cooking and Attitudes Using Time-Use Diary Data." In *Food, Masculinities and Home: Interdisciplinary Perspectives*, edited by Michelle Szabo and Shelley Koch, 31–58. London: Bloomsbury.

Danizer, Pamela. 2018. "Online Grocery Sales to Reach $100 Billion in 2025; Amazon Is Current and Future Leader." *Forbes*. January 18, 2018. Accessed September 27, 2018. https://www.forbes.com/sites/pamdanziger/2018/01/18/online-grocery-sales-to-reach-100-billion-in-2025-amazon-set-to-be-market-share-leader/#113b207162f3.

Dean, Stacy and Dorothy Rosenbaum. 2013. "SNAP Benefits Will Be Cut for All Participants in November 2013." Center on Budget and Policy Priories. Accessed March 2014. http://www.cbpp.org/cms/?fa=view&id=3899.

DeLind, Laura and Anne Ferguson. 1999. "Is This a Women's Movement? The Relationship of Gender to Community-Supported Agriculture in Michigan." *Human Organization* 58(2): 190–200.

Deutsch, Jonathan. 2005. "Please Pass the Chicken Tits: Rethinking Men and Cooking at an Urban Firehouse." *Food and Foodways* 13(1): 91–114.

Deutsch, Tracey. 2012. *Building a Housewife's Paradise: Gender, Politics, and American Grocery Stores in the Twentieth Century*. Chapel Hill: University of North Carolina Press.

DeVault, Marjorie. 1991. *Feeding the Family*. Chicago: University of Chicago Press.

Devine, C. M., M. Jastran, J. Jabs, E. Wethington, T. J. Farell, and C. A. Bisogni. 2006. "A Lot of Sacrifices: Work-Family Spillover and the Food Choice Coping Strategies of Low-Wage Employed Parents." *Social Science and Medicine* 63(10): 2591–2603.

Devlin, Claire and Robert Elgie. 2008. "The Effect of Increased Women's Representation in Parliament: The Case of Rwanda." *Parliamentary Affairs* 61(2): 237–254.

Dixon, Jane. 2007. "Supermarkets as New Food Authorites." In *Supermarkets and Agri-food Supply Chains: Transformations in the Production and Consumption of Food*, by D. Burch and G. Lawrence, 20–50. Cheltenham, UK: Edward Elgar.

———. 2008. "Operating Upstream and Downstream: How Supermarkets Exercise Power in the Food System." In *A Sociology of Food and Nutrition*, by J. Germov and L. Williams, 100–123. Melbourne, Australia: Oxford University Press.

Dixon, Jane and Kathy Banwell. 2004. "Re-embedding Trust: Unravelling the Construction of Modern Diets." *Journal of Critical Public Health* 14(2): 117–131.

Dixon, Jane, Abiud M. Omwega, Sharon Friel, Cate Burns, Kelly Donati, and Rachel Carlisle. 2007. "The Health Equity Dimensions of Urban Food Systems." *Journal of Urban Health: Bulletin of the New York Academy of Medicine* 84: 118–129.

Dolan, Catherine S. 2005. "Benevolent Intent? The Development Encounter in Kenya's Horticulture Industry." *Journal of Asian and African Studies* 40(6): 411–437.

Donham, K. J. and A. Thelin. 2006. *Agricultural Medicine: Occupational and Environmental Health for the Health Professions*. Ames, IA: Blackwell.

Duffy, Mignon. 2005. "Reproducing Labor Inequalities: Challenges for Feminists Conceptualizing Care at the Intersections of Gender, Race, and Class." *Gender and Society* 19(1): 66–82.

———. 2007. "Doing the Dirty Work: Gender, Race and Reproductive Labor in Historical Perspective." *Gender and Society* 21(3): 313–336.

DuPuis, Melanie E. 2015. *Dangerous Digestion: The Politics of American Dietary Advice*. Berkeley: University of California Press.

Edin, Kathryn and Laura Lein. 1997. *Making Ends Meet: How Single Mothers Survive Welfare and Low-Wage Work*. New York: Russell Sage Foundation.

Elliott, Sinikka and Sarah Bowen. 2018. "Defending Motherhood: Morality, Responsibility, and Double Binds in Feeding Children." *Journal of Marriage and Family* 80: 499–520. doi: 10.1111/jomf.12465.

Ellis, R. 1983. "The Way to a Man's Heart: Food in the Violent Home." In *The Sociology of Food and Eating: Essays in the Sociological Significance of Food*, edited by A. Murcott, 164–171. Aldershot, UK: Gower.

England, Paula. 2010. "The Gender Revolution: Uneven and Stalled." *Gender and Society* 24: 149–166.

England, Paula and George Farkas. 1986. *Households, Employment and Gender: A Social, Economic and Demographic View*. New York: Aldine.

England, Paula and Nancy Folbre. 1999. "The Cost of Caring." *Annals of the American Academy of Political and Social Science* 56: 39–51.

Equal Employment Opportunity Commission (EEOC). 2015. "EEOC Wins Jury Verdict of Over $17 Million for Victims of Sexual Harassment and Retaliation at Moreno Farm." EEOC. Accessed April 10, 2016. https://www1.eeoc.gov/eeoc/newsroom/release/9-10-15.cfm.

Erosion, Technology and Concentration (ETC) Group. 2005. "Global Seed Industry Concentration—2005." Issue #90. ETC Group. Accessed January 2016. http://www.etcgroup.org/sites/www.etcgroup.org/files/publication/48/01/seedmaster fin2005.pdf.

Featherstone, L. 2004. *Selling Women Short: The Landmark Battle in Workers' Rights at Wal-Mart*. New York: Basic Books.

Federici, Silvia. 2009. "On Capitalism, Colonialism, Women and Food Politics." *Politics and Culture*, issue 2. Accessed November 2017. https://politicsandculture.org/2009/11/03/silvia-federici-on-capitalism-colonialism-women-and-food-politics.

Ferrell, Anne. 2012. "Doing Masculinity: Gendered Challenges to Replacing Burley Tobacco in Central Kentucky." *Agriculture and Human Values* 29: 137–149.

Fink, Deborah. 1992. *Agrarian Women: Wives and Mothers in Rural Nebraska, 1880–1940*. Chapel Hill: University of North Carolina Press.

Fisher, Andrew. 2017. *Big Hunger: The Unholy Alliance Between Corporate America and Anti-hunger Groups*. Cambridge, MA: MIT Press.

Flagg, Lee Anne, Sen Bisakha, Meredith L. Kilgore, and Julie L. Locher. 2014. "The Influence of Gender, Age, Education, and Household Size on Meal Preparation and Food Shopping Responsibilities." *Public Health Nutrition* 17(9): 2061–2070.

Flegal, K. M., B. I. Graubard, D. F. Williamson, and M. H. Gail. 2005. "Excess Deaths Associated with Underweight, Overweight, and Obesity." *American Medical Association* 293(15): 1861–1867.

Folbre, Nancy. 1991. "The Unproductive Housewife: Her Evolution in Nineteenth-Century Economic Thought." *Signs* 16(3): 463–484.

Foley, Johnathan. 2013. "It's Time to Rethink America's Corn System." *Scientific American*. March 13. Accessed March 25, 2015. https://www.scientificamerican.com/article/time-to-rethink-corn.

Food and Agriculture Organization (FAO). 2011. "The State of Food and Agriculture: Women in Agriculture: Closing the Gender Gap for Development." Accessed May 10, 2015. http://www.fao.org/docrep/013/i2050e/i2050e.pdf.

———. 2017. "The State of Food Security and Nutrition in the World." FAO. Accessed May 2018. http://www.fao.org/3/a-I7695e.pdf.

Food Chain Workers Alliance (FCWA). 2012. "The Hands That Feed Us." FCWA. Accessed June 2014. http://foodchainworkers.org/wp-content/uploads/2012/06/Hands-That-Feed-Us-Report.pdf.

Food Chain Workers Alliance and Solidarity Research Cooperative. 2016. *No Piece of the Pie: U.S. Food Workers in 2016*. Los Angeles, CA: Food Chain Workers Alliance.

Food Marketing Institute (FMI). 2015. "Supermarket Facts." FMI. Accessed June 2014. http://www.fmi.org/research-resources/supermarket-facts.

Frye, Joselyn. 2017. "Not Just the Rich and Famous." Center for American Progress. November 20, 2017. Accessed May 2018. https://www.americanprogress.org/issues/women/news/2017/11/20/443139/not-just-rich-famous.

Furst, E. 1997. "Cooking and Femininity." *Women's Studies International Forum* 20(3): 441–449.

Galarneau, Charlene. 2013. "Farm Labor, Reproductive Justice: Migrant Women Farmworkers in the U.S." *Health and Human Rights* 15: 1.

Gettman, H. J. and M. J. Gelfand. 2007. "When the Customer Shouldn't Be King: Antecedents and Consequences of Sexual Harassment by Clients and Customers." *Journal of Applied Psychology* 92(3): 757–770.

Glass, Jennifer and Valerie Camarigg. 1992. "Gender, Parenthood, and Job-Family Compatibility." *American Journal of Sociology* 98(1): 131–151.

Glazer, Nona. 1990. *Women's Paid and Unpaid Labor: The Work Transfer in Health Care and Retailing*. Philadelphia: Temple University Press.

Glover, T. D., K. J. Shinew, and D. C. Parry. 2005. "Association, Sociability, and Civic Culture: The Democratic Effect of Community Gardening." *Leisure Sciences* 27(1): 75–92.

Glucksman, Miriam. 1995. "Why 'Work'? Gender and the Total Organization of Labor." *Gender, Work and Organization* 2(2): 63–75.

Goldberg, Abbie E., Julianna Smith, and Maureen Perry-Jenkins. 2012. "The Division of Labor in Lesbian, Gay, and Heterosexual New Adoptive Parents." *Journal of Marriage and Family* 74(4): 812–828.

Goodman, David and Michael Redclift. 1991. *Refashioning Nature: Food, Ecology, and Culture*. New York: Routledge.

Goodman, Jack. 2016. "Who Does the Grocery Shopping, and When Do They Do It?" Time Use Institute. Accessed April 15, 2015. www.timeuseinstitute.org/Grocery16paper.pdf.

Gorman-Murray, Andrew. 2008. "Masculinity and the Home: A Critical Review and Conceptual Framework." *Australian Geographer* 39(3): 367–379.

Gortmaker, S. L., A. Must, J. M. Perrin, A. M. Sobol, and W. H. Dietz. 1993. "Social and Economic Consequences of Overweight in Adolescence and Young Adulthood." *New England Journal of Medicine* 329: 1008–1012.

Gottlieb, Robert and Anupama Joshi. 2010. *Food Justice*. Cambridge, MA: MIT Press.

Gough, Brendan. 2007. "Real Men Don't Diet: An Analysis of Contemporary Newspaper Presentations of Men, Food, and Health." *Social Science and Medicine* 64: 326–337.

Gouveia, Lourdes and Arunas Juska. 2002. "Taming Nature, Taming Workers: Constructing the Separation Between Meat Consumption and Meat Production in the U.S." *Sociologia Ruralis* 42(4): 370–390.

Guiffre, Patti and Christine Williams. 1994. "Boundary Lines: Labeling Sexual Harassment in Restaurants." *Gender and Society* 8(3): 378–401.

Gupta, S. 1999. "The Effects of Transitions in Marital Status on Men's Performance of Housework." *Journal of Marriage and Family* 61: 700–711.

Guthman, Julie. 2008a. "Bringing Good Food to Others: Investigating the Subjects of Alternative Food Practice." *Cultural Geographies* 15: 431–447.

———. 2008b. "'If They Only Knew': Color Blindness and Universalism in California Alternative Food Institutions." *Professional Geographer* 60: 387–397.

———. 2011. *Obesity, Food Justice, and the Limits of Capitalism*. Berkeley: University of California Press.

Guthman, Julie and Melanie DuPuis. 2006. "Embodying Neoliberalism: Economy, Culture, and the Politics of Fat." *Environment and Planning D: Society and Space* 24: 427–448.

Hales, C. M., M. D. Carroll, C. D. Fryar, and C. L. Ogden. 2017. "Prevalence of Obesity among Adults and Youth: United States, 2015–2016." NCHS Data Brief 288. Hyattsville, MD: National Center for Health Statistics.

Hall, Alan and Veronika Mogyorody. 2007. "Organic Farming, Gender, and the Labor Process." *Rural Sociology* 72(2): 289–316.

Hamerschlag, Kari and Stacy Malkan. N.d. "Spinning Food: How Food Industry Front Groups and Covert Communications Are Shaping the Story of Food." Friends of the Earth. Accessed April 13, 2017. https://foe.org/resources/spinning -food-how-food-industry-front-groups-and-covert-communications-are-shaping -the-story-of-food.

Hamrick, Karen, Margaret Andrews, Joanne Guthrie, David Hopkins, and Ket McCelland. 2011. "How Much Time Do Americans Spend on Food?" Economic Information Bulletin 86. Washington DC: USDA-ERS.

Harding, Sandra. 1986. *The Science Question in Feminism*. Ithaca, NY: Cornell University Press.

Harris, Deborah and Patti Guiffre. 2015. *Taking the Heat: Women Chefs and Gender Inequality in the Professional Kitchen*. New Brunswick, NJ: Rutgers University Press.

Harvey, David. 2005. *A Brief History of Neoliberalism*. New York: Oxford University Press.

Hassanein, Neva. 1999. *Changing the Way America Farms: Knowledge and Community in the Sustainable Agriculture Movement*. Lincoln: University of Nebraska Press.

Haugen, Madt S. 1998. "The Gendering of Farming: The Case of Norway." *European Journal of Women's Studies* 5(2): 133–153.

Hayes, Sharon. 1996. *The Cultural Contradictions of Motherhood*. Cambridge, MA: Yale University Press.

Hayes-Conroy, Alison and Jessica Hayes-Conroy. 2013. "Feminist Nutrition: Difference, Decolonization, and Dietary Change." In *Doing Nutrition Differently: Critical Approaches to Diet and Dietary Intervention*, edited by Allison Hayes-Conroy and Jessica Hayes-Conroy, 173–188. Burlington, VT: Ashgate Publishing Company.

Hayes-Conroy, Jessica, Nancy Chen, and Aya H. Kimura. 2014. "Other Ways of Knowing." *Gastronomica: The Journal of Critical Food Studies* 14(3): 27–35.

Heflin, Colleen, Andrew S. London, and Ellen K. Scott. 2011. "Mitigating Material Hardship: The Strategies Low-Income Families Employ to Reduce the Consequences of Poverty." *Sociological Inquiry* 81(2): 223–246.

Heldke, Lisa. 2013. "Let's Cook Thai: Recipes for Colonialism." In *Food and Culture: A Reader*, edited by Carole Counihan and Penny Van Esterik, 394–408. New York: Routledge.

Hendrickson, Mary and William Heffernan. 2007. "Concentration of Agricultural Markets." Food Circles Networking Project. Accessed October 12, 2016. www .foodcircles.missouri.edu/07contable.pdf.

Hepworth, J. 2008. "The Social Construction of Eating Disorders." In *A Sociology of Food and Nutrition: The Social Appetite*, edited by J. Germov and L. Williams. 3rd ed. Melbourne, Australia: Oxford University Press.

Hill Collins, Patricia. 2000. *Black Feminist Thought, Knowledge, Consciousness, and the Politics of Empowerment*. New York: Routledge.

Hinrichs, Clarie. 2000. "Embeddedness and Local Food Systems: Notes of Two Types of Direct Agricultural Markets." *Journal of Rural Studies* 16(3): 295–303.

Hochschild, Arlie Russell. 1983. *The Managed Heart: Commercialization of Human Feeling*. Berkeley: University of California Press.

Hockey, J., A. Meah, and V. Robinson. 2007. *Mundane Heterosexualities: From Theory to Practice*. Basingstoke, UK: Palgrave MacMillan.

Hollows, Joanne. 2003. "Oliver's Twist: Leisure, Labour and Domestic Masculinity in The Naked Chef." *International Journal of Cultural Studies* 6(2): 229–248.

Holt-Gimenez, Eric. 2017. *A Foodie's Guide to Capitalism: Understanding the Political Economy of What We Eat*. New York: Monthly Review Press.

Hondagneu-Sotelo, Pierrette. 2000. "Feminism and Migration Scholarship." *Annals of the American Academy of Political and Social Science* 571: 107–120.

Hook, Jennifer. 2006. "Care in Context: Men's Unpaid Work in 20 Countries, 1965–2003." *American Sociological Review* 71(4): 639–660.

hooks, bell. 1990. *Yearning: Race, Gender and Cultural Politics*. Boston: South End Press.

———. 1992. "Eating the Other: Desire and Resistance." *Black Looks: Race and Representation*. Boston: South End Books.

Hoppe, R. A. and P. Korb. 2013. "Characteristics of Women Farm Operators and Their Farms." Economic Information Bulletin 111. U.S. Department of Agriculture, Economic Research Service. Accessed November 17, 2015. https://papers.ssrn.com/sol3/papers.cfm?abstract_id=2266538.

Hovorka, Alice J. 1998. "Gender Resources for Development Research and Programming in Urban Agriculture." Cities Feeding People Series, Report No. 26. Ottawa, Canada: IDRC.

Hudson, J. I., E. Hiripi, H. G. Pope, and R. C. Kessler. 2007. "The Prevalence and Correlates of Eating Disorder Statistics in the National Comorbidity Survey Replication." *Biological Psychiatry* 61(3): 348–358.

Hughes, K. and V. Tadic. 1998. "Something to Deal With: Customer Sexual Harassment and Women's Retail Service Work in Canada." *Gender, Work and Organization* 5(4): 207–219.

Humphery, Kim. 1998. *Shelf Life: Supermarkets and the Changing Cultures of Consumption*. Cambridge: Cambridge University Press.

Hurni, H. and B. Osman-Elasha. 2009. "Context, Conceptual Framework and Sustainability Indicators." In *Agriculture at a Crossroads: Global Report*, edited by B. D. McIntyre, H. R. Herran, J. Wakhungu, and R. T. Watson. Washington, DC: International Assessment of Agricultural Knowledge, Science and Technology for Development.

Hyder, A., S. Maman, J. Nyoni, S. Khasiani, N. Teoh, Z. Premji, and S. Sohani. 2005. "The Pervasive Triad of Food Security, Gender Inequity and Women's Health: Exploratory Research from Sub-Saharan Africa." *African Health Sciences* 5(4): 328–334.

Inness, Sherrie A. 2001. *Kitchen Culture in America: Popular Representations of Food, Gender, and Race*. Philadelphia: University of Pennsylvania.

Intergovernmental Panel on Climate Change. 2014. *Climate Change 2014: Mitigation of Climate Change. Contribution of Working Group III to the Fifth Assessment Report of the Intergovernmental Panel on Climate Change*. Cambridge: Cambridge University Press.

Jabs, J., C. Devine, A. Bisogni, T. Farrell, M. Jastran, and E. Wetherington. 2007. "Trying to Find the Quickest Way: Employed Mothers' Constructions of Time for Food." *Journal of Nutrition Education and Behavior* 39(1): 18–25.

Jacobs, Andrew, and Matt Richtel. 2017. "How Big Business Got Brazil Hooked on Junk Food." *New York Times*. September 16. https://www.nytimes.com/interactive/2017/09/16/health/brazil-obesity-nestle.html

Jacobs, Anna W. and Irene Padavic. 2015. "Hours, Scheduling and Flexibility for Women in the US Low-Wage Labour Force." *Gender, Work and Organization* 22(1): 67–86.

Jayaraman, Saru. 2013. *Behind the Kitchen Door*. Ithaca, NY: Cornell University Press.

Jensen, Joan M. 1986. *Loosening the Bonds: Mid-Atlantic Farm Women, 1750–1850*. New Haven, CT: Yale University Press.

Jensen, K. O. and L. Holm. 1999. "Preferences, Quantities and Concerns: Socio-cultural Perspectives on the Gendered Consumption of Foods." *European Journal of Clinical Nutrition* 53: 351–359. doi: 10.1038/sj.ejcn.1600767.

Johansson, Kristina and Anna Sofia Lundgren. 2015. "Gendering Boundary Work: Exploring Excluded Spaces in Supermarket Job Rotation." *Gender, Place and Culture* 22(2): 188–204.

Johnston, Josee and Shyon Baumann. 2010. *Foodies: Democracy and Distinction in the Gourmet Foodscape*. New York: Routledge.

Julier, Alice. 2013. "The Political Economy of Obesity: The Fat Pay All." *In Food and Culture: A Reader*, edited by Carole Counihan and Penny Van Esterik, 546–562. New York: Routledge.

Kan, M. Y., O. Sullivan, and J. Gershuny. 2011. "Gender Convergence in Domestic Work: Discerning the Effects of Interactional and Institutional Barriers from Large-Scale Data." *Sociology* 45: 234–251.

Karpf, Sheila. 2011. "Women in Agriculture, by the Numbers." Civil Eats. Accessed January 2014. https://civileats.com/2011/02/25/women-in-agriculture-by-the-numbers.

Keith-Jennings, Brynne and Raheem Chaudhry. 2018. "Most Working-Age SNAP Participants Work, but Often in Unstable Jobs." Center on Budget and Policy Priorities. Accessed May 14, 2018. https://www.cbpp.org/research/food-assistance/most-working-age-snap-participants-work-but-often-in-unstable-jobs.

Kennedy, Scott Hamilton, dir. 2009. *The Garden*. New York: Oscilloscop Laboratories.

Koch, Shelley L. 2012. *A Theory of Grocery Shopping: Food, Choice and Conflict*. London: Berg.

Kreider, R. M. and R. Ellis. 2011. "Living Arrangements of Children: 2009." Current Population Reports P70-126. U.S. Census Bureau. Accessed March 13, 2017. http://www.census.gov/prod/2011pubs/p70-126.pdf.

Kritzinger, Andrienetta, Stephanie Barrientos, and Hester Rossouw. 2004. "Global Production and Flexible Employment in South African Horticulture: Experiences of Contract Workers in Fruit Exports." *Sociologia Ruralis* 44(1): 17–39.

Kurdek, Lawrence A. 2007. "The Allocation of Household Labor by Partners in Gay and Lesbian Couples." *Journal of Family Issues* 28(1): 132–148.

LeBesco, Kathleen. 2004. *Revolting Bodies? The Struggle to Redefine Fat Identity*. Amherst: University of Massachusetts Press.

Leckie, Gloria J. 1996. "Female Farmers in Canada and the Gender Relations of a Restructuring Agricultural System." *Canadian Geographer/Le géographe canadien* 37(3): 212–230.

Lee, Richard B. 1979. *The !Kung San: Men, Women, and Work in a Foraging Society.* Cambridge: Cambridge University Press.

Lee, Sang E. 2010. "Unpacking the Packing Plant: Nicaraguan Migrant Women's Work in Costa Rica's Evolving Export Agriculture Sector." *Signs* 35(2): 317–342.

Levanon, Asaf, Paula England, and Paul Allison. 2009. "Occupational Feminization and Pay: Assessing Causal Dynamics Using 1950–2000 U.S. Census Data." *Social Forces* 88(2): 865–891.

Levi-Strauss, Claude. 1964. *The Raw and the Cooked.* New York: Harper and Row.

Liepins, Ruth. 1998. "The Gendering of Farming and Agricultural Policies: A Matter of Discourse and Power." *Australian Geographer* 29(3): 371–388.

Little, J., B. Ibery, and D. Watts. 2009. "Gender, Consumption, and the Relocalization of Food: A Research Agenda." *Sociologia Ruralis* 49(3): 201–217.

Lupton, Deborah. 1996. *Food, Body and the Self.* London: Sage.

———. 2000. "'Where's Me Dinner?' Food Preparation Arrangements in Rural Australian Families." *Journal of Sociology* 36(2): 172–186.

Lyons, Pat. 2009. "Prescription for Harm: Diet Industry Influence, Public Health Policy and the 'Obesity Epidemic.'" In *The Fat Studies Reader*, edited by Esther Rothblum and Sondra Solovay, 75–87. New York: New York University Press.

Macintosh, Alison A., Ron Pinhasi, and Jay T. Stock. 2017. "Prehistoric Women's Manual Labor Exceeded That of Athletes Through the First 5500 Years of Farming in Central Europe." *Science Advances* 3(11). doi: 10.1126/sciadv.aao3893.

Mackendrick, Norah. 2014. "More Work for Mother: Chemical Body Burdens as a Maternal Responsibility." *Gender and Society* 28(5): 1–24.

Magdoff, Fred. 2012. "Food as a Commodity." *Monthly Review* 63(8) (January).

Mammon, Kristin and Christina Paxon. 2000. "Women's Work and Economic Development." *Journal of Economic Perspectives* 14(4): 141–164.

Mancino, Lisa and Constance Newman. 2007. "Who Has Time to Cook? How Family Resources Influence Food Preparation." Economic Research Report Number 40. U.S. Department of Agriculture, Economic Research Service. Accessed January 28, 2015. https://www.ers.usda.gov/publications/pub-details/?pubid=45800.

Mannon, Susan, Peggy Petrzelka, Christy M. Glass, and Claudia Radel. 2011. "Keeping Them in Their Place: Migrant Women Workers in Spain's Strawberry Industry." *International Journal of the Sociology of Agriculture and Food* 19(1): 83–101.

Martin, M. A. and A. M. Lippert. 2012. "Feeding Her Children, but Risking Her Health: The Intersection of Gender, Household Food Insecurity and Obesity." *Social Science and Medicine* 74(11): 1754–1764.

Maume, David J., Rachel A. Sebastian, and Anthony R. Bardo. 2010. "Gender, Work-Family Responsibilities, and Sleep." *Gender and Society* 24(1): 746–768.

McCurdy, S. A. and D. J. Carroll. 2000. "Agricultural Injury." *American Journal of Industrial Medicine* 38(4): 463–480.

McIntosh, W. and M. Zey. 1990. "Women as Gatekeepers of Food Consumption: A Sociological Critique." *Food and Foodways* 34(4): 317–332.

McIntosh, W. L., E. Spies, D. M. Stone, C. N. Lokey, A. T. Trudeau, and B. Bartholow. 2016. "Suicide Rates by Occupational Group—17 States, 2012." *Morbidity and*

Mortality Weekly Report 65: 641–645. doi: http://dx.doi.org/10.15585/mmwr.mm6525a1.

McIntyre, L. and K. Rondeau. 2011. "Individual Consumer Food Localism: A Review Anchored in Canadian Farmwomen's Reflections." *Journal of Rural Studies* 27(2): 116–124.

McIntyre, Lynn N., Theresa Glanville, Kim D. Raine, Jutta B. Dayle, Bonnie Anderson, and Noreen Battaglia. 2003. "Do Low-Income Lone Mothers Compromise Their Nutrition to Feed Their Children?" *Canadian Medical Association Journal* 168(6): 686–691.

McKie, Linda, Gill Hogg, Laura Airey, Kathryn Backett-Milburn, and Zoe Rew. 2009. "Autonomy, Control and Job Advancement: The Case of Low Paid Women Working in Food Retail." *Work, Employment & Society* 23(4): 787–796.

Meah, Angela. 2014. "Reconceptualizing Power and Gendered Subjectivities in Domestic Cooking Spaces." *Progress in Human Geography* 38(5): 671–690.

Meah, Angela and Peter Jackson. 2013. "Crowded Kitchens: The 'Democratisation' of Domesticity?" *Gender, Place and Culture: A Journal of Feminist Geography* 20(5): 578–596.

Meares, Alison. 1997. "Making the Transition from Conventional to Sustainable Agriculture: Gender, Social Movement Participation and the Quality of Life on the Family Farm." *Rural Sociology* 62(1): 21–47.

Mechling, Jay. 2005. "Boy Scouts and the Manly Art of Cooking." *Food and Foodways* 13(1): 67–89.

Mennell, S., A. Murcott, and A. H. Otterloo. 1992. *The Sociology of Food: Eating, Diet, and Culture*. London: Sage.

Mennell, Stephen. 1995. *All Manners of Food: Eating and Taste in England and France from the Middle Ages to the Present*. Oxford, UK: Blackwell.

Merchant, Carolyn. 1980. *The Death of Nature: Women, Ecology and the Scientific Revolution*. New York: HarperCollins.

———. 1989. *Ecological Revolutions: Nature, Gender, and Science in New England*. Chapel Hill: University of North Carolina Press.

Metcalfe, A., C. Dryden, M. Johnson, J. Owen, and G. Shipton. 2009. "Fathers, Food and Family Life." In *Changing Families, Changing Food*, edited by P. Jackson, 93–117. Basingstoke, UK: Palgrave Macmillan.

Mies, Maria. 1993. "Feminist Research: Science, Violence, and Responsibility." In *Ecofeminism*, edited by Maria Mies and Vandana Shiva, 36–54. London: Zed Books.

Miller, Daniel. 1998. *A Theory of Shopping*. Ithaca, NY: Cornell University Press.

Miranda, Veerle. 2011. "Cooking, Caring and Volunteering: Unpaid Work Around the World." OECD Social, Employment and Migration Working Papers no. 116. Paris: OECD Publishing. doi: 10.1787/5kghrjm8s142-en.

Mori, D., S. Chaiken, and P. Pliner. 1987. "'Eating Lightly' and the Self-Presentation of Femininity." *Journal of Perspectives in Social Psychology* 53(4): 693–702.

Morrison, Rosanna Mentzer and Lisa Mancino. 2015. "Most U.S. Households Do Their Main Grocery Shopping at Supermarkets and Supercenters Regardless of Income." Amber Waves. Accessed February 5, 2016. http://www.ers.usda.gov/amber-waves/2015-august/most-us-households-do-their-main-grocery-shopping-at-supermarkets-and-supercenters-regardless-of-income.aspx#.V87QMvkrJD8.

Moss, Michael. 2009. "Peanut Case Shows Holes in the Safety Net." *New York Times*. https://www.nytimes.com/2009/02/09/us/09peanuts.html.

MRI. 2008. Nationale Verzehrsstudie II—Ergebnisbericht, Teil 2—Die bundesweite Befragung zur Ernährung von Jugendlichen und Erwachsenen. Karlsruhe, Germany: Max Rubner Institute, 174–234.

Mroz, Lawrence W., Gwen E. Chapman, John L. Oliffe, and Joan L. Bottorff. 2011. "Men, Food, and Prostate Cancer: Gender Influences on Men's Diets." *American Journal of Men's Health* 5(2) 177–187.

Mudry, Jessica. 2009. *Measured Meals: Nutrition in America*. Albany: State University of New York.

Mudry, Jessica, Jessica Hayes-Conroy, Nancy Chen, and Aya H. Kimura. 2014. "Other Ways of Knowing Food." *Gastronomica: The Journal of Food and Culture* 14(3): 27–23.

Mundy, A. 2010. *Dispensing with the Truth: The Victims, the Drug Companies, and the Dramatic Story Behind the Battle over Fen-Phen*. New York: St. Martin's Press.

Mundy, L. 2013. "The Gay Guide to Wedding Bliss." *The Atlantic* 317(5): 56–70.

Murcott, A. 1982. "On the Social Significance of the 'Cooked Dinner' in South Wales." *Social Science Information* 21(4/5): 677–695.

———. 1983. "'It's a Pleasure to Cook for Him': Food, Meal Times and Gender in South Wales Households." In *The Public and the Private*, edited by E. Gamarnikow, D. Morgan, J. Purvis, and D. Taylorson, 78–90. London: Heinemann.

Murdock, G. P. and C. Provost. 1973. "Factors in the Division of Labor by Sex: A Cross-Cultural Analysis." *Ethnology* 12(2): 203–225.

Murphy, Elizabeth. 2008. "Risk, Maternal Ideologies and Infant Feeding." In *A Sociology of Food and Nutrition: The Social Appetite*, edited by John Germov and Lauren Williams, 205–223. 3rd ed. South Melbourne, Australia: Oxford University Press.

Naccarato, Peter and Kathleen LeBesco. 2012. *Culinary Capital*. Oxford, UK: Berg.

Nath, J. 2011. "Gendered Fare? A Qualitative Investigation of Alternative Food and Masculinities." *Journal of Sociology* 47: 261–278. doi: 10.1177/1440783310386828.

National Science Foundation (NSF). 2006. "Women, Minorities, and Persons with Disabilities in Science and Engineering." NSF. http://www.nsf.gov/statistics.

Nelson, Julie. 1993. "A Study of Choice or the Study of Provisioning? Gender and the Definition of Economics." In *Beyond Economic Man: Feminist Theory and Economics*, edited by Marianne A. Ferber and Julie A. Nelson. Chicago: University of Chicago Press.

Neuhaus, Jessamyn. 2003. *Manly Meals and Mom's Home Cooking: Cookbooks and Gender in Modern America*. Baltimore: John Hopkins University Press.

Neumark-Sztainer, D., M. Wall, N. I. Larson, M. E. Eisenberg, and K. Loth. 2011. "Dieting and Disordered Eating Behaviors from Adolescence to Young Adulthood: Findings from a 10-Year Longitudinal Study." *Journal of the American Dietetic Association* 111(7): 1004–1011.

Newman, Katherine S. and Rourke L. O'Brien. 2011. *Taxing the Poor: Doing Damage to the Truly Disadvantaged*. Berkeley: University of California Press.

Nilsson, Gabriella. 2013. "Balls Enough: Manliness and Legitimated Violence in Hell's Kitchen." *Gender, Work and Organization* 20(6): 647–663.

Nord, Mark, Margaret Andrews, and Steven Carlson. 2009. "Household Food Security in the United States, 2008." ERR-83. U.S. Department of Agriculture, Economic Research Service. Accessed May 2015. http://www.ers.usda.gov/publications/err83.

O'Dea, J. A. and S. Abraham. 2002. "Eating and Exercise Disorders in Young College Men." *Journal of American College Health* 50: 273–277.

Ogden, C. L., M. M. Lamb, M. D. Carroll, and K. M. Flegal. 2010. "Obesity and Socioeconomic Status in Adults: United States 1988–1994 and 2005–2008." NCHS Data Brief 50. Hyattsville, MD: National Center for Health Statistics.

Ontiveros, Maria. 2003. "Lessons from the Fields: Female Farmworkers and the Law." *Maine Law Review* 55(1): 169.

Orbach, Susie. 1978. *Fat Is a Feminist Issue*. London: Hamlyn.

Ore, Tracy E. 2011. "Something from Nothing: Women, Space, and Resistance." *Gender and Society* 25(6): 689–695.

Organo, Vanessa, Leslie Head, and Gordon Waitt. 2013. "Who Does the Work in Sustainable Households? A Time and Gender Analysis in New South Wales, Australia." *Gender, Place and Culture* 20(5): 559–577.

Owen, J., A. Metcalfe, C. Dryden, and D. Shipton. 2010. "If They Don't Eat It, It's Not a Proper Meal: Images of Risk and Choice in Fathers' Accounts of Family Food Practices." *Health, Risk and Society* 12(4): 395–406.

Paquette, Marie-Claude and Kim Raine. 2004. "Sociocultural Context of Women's Body Image." *Social Science and Medicine* 59: 1047–1058.

Parasecoli, Fabio. 2005. "Feeding Hard Bodies: Food and Masculinities in Men's Fitness Magazines." *Food and Foodways* 13(1–2): 17–37.

Parsons, Julie. 2014. *Gender, Class and Food: Families, Bodies and Health*. Basingstoke, UK: Palgrave Macmillan.

Patel, Raj. 2012. *Stuffed and Starved: The Hidden Battle for the World Food System*. 2nd ed. Brooklyn, NY: Melville House Publishing.

Peter, Gregory, Michael Mayerfeld Bell, Susan Jarnagin, and Donna Bauer. 2000. "Coming Back Across the Fence: Masculinity and the Transition to Sustainable Agriculture." *Rural Sociology* 65(2): 215–233.

Peterman, A., A. Quisumbing, and J. Behrman. 2010. "A Review of Empirical Evidence on Gender Differences in Non-land Agricultural Inputs, Technology, and Services in Developing Countries." Paper prepared for the State of Food and Agriculture, 2010–2011. Rome, FAO.

Peters, Virginia. 1995. *Women of the Earth Lodges: Tribal Life on the Plains*. North Haven, CT: Archon Books.

Pilgeram, Ryanne and Bryan Amos. 2015. "Beyond 'Inherit It or Marry It': Exploring How Women Engaged in Sustainable Agriculture Access Farmland." *Rural Sociology* 80(1): 16–38. doi: 10.1111/ruso.12054.

Pini, Barbara. 2005. "The Third Sex: Women Leaders in Australian Agriculture." *Gender, Work and Organization* 12(1): 73–88.

Pope, H. G., Jr., R. Olivardia, A. Gruber, and J. Borowiecki. 1999. "Evolving Ideals of Male Body Image as Seen Through Action Toys." *International Journal of Eating Disorders* 26: 65–72.

Preibisch, Kerry and Evelyn Encalada Grez. 2010. "The Other Side of el Otro Lado: Mexican Migrant Women and Labor Flexibility in Canadian Agriculture." *Signs* 35(2): 289–316.

Preibisch, Kerry and Luz María Hermoso Santamaría. 2006. "Engendering Labour Migration: The Case of Foreign Workers in Canadian Agriculture." In *Women, Migration and Citizenship: Making Local, National and Transnational Connections,* edited by Evangelia Tastsoglou and Alexandra Dobrowolsky, 107–130. Aldershot, UK: Ashgate.

Puhl, Rebecca, Tatiana Andreyeva, and Kelly Brownell. 2008. "Perceptions of Weight Discrimination: Prevalence and Comparison to Race and Gender Discrimination in America." *International Journal of Obesity* 32: 992–1000.

Ray, K. 2004. *The Migrant's Table: Meals and Memories in Bengali-American Households.* Philadelphia: Temple University Press.

Reardon, Thomas, C. Peter Timmer, Christopher B. Barrett, and Julio Berdegue. 2003. "The Rise of Supermarkets in Africa, Asia, and Latin America." *American Journal of Agricultural Economics* 85: 1140–1146.

Renting, H., I. Marsden, and J. Banks. 2003. "Understanding Alternative Food Networks: Exploring the Role of Short Food Supply Chains in Rural Development." *Environment and Planning A* 35: 393–411.

Reschke, K. L. 2012. "Child Care Needs of Farm Families." *Journal of Agromedicine* 17(2): 208–213.

Restaurant Opportunities Centers United. 2013. "The Third Shift: Child Care Needs and Access for Working Mothers in Restaurants." ROC United. Accessed May 14, 2016. http://rocunited.org/wp-content/uploads/2013/11/reports_third-shift-final-mm.pdf.

———. 2014. "The Glass Floor: Sexual Harassment in the Restaurant Industry." ROC United. Accessed May 23, 2016. http://rocunited.org/wp-content/uploads/2014/10/REPORT_TheGlassFloor_Sexual-Harassment-in-the-Restaurant-Industry.pdf.

———. 2015. "Ending Jim Crow in America's Restaurants: Racial and Gender Occupational Segregation in the Restaurant Industry." ROC United. http://rocunited.org/wp content/uploads/2015/10/RaceGender_Report_LR.pdf.

Rice, Julie Steinkopf. 2015. "Privilege and Exclusion at the Farmers Market: Findings from a Survey of Shoppers." *Agriculture and Human Values* 10: 21–29.

Richards, Carol, Geoffry Lawrence, and David Burch. 2011. "Supermarkets and Agro-industrial Foods: The Strategic Manufacturing of Consumer Trust." *Food, Culture and Society* 14(1): 29–47.

Rodney, Alexandra, Josee Johnston, and Phillipa Chong. 2017. "Chefs at Home? Masculinities on Offer in Celebrity Chef Cookbooks." In *Food, Masculinities and Home: Interdisciplinary Perspectives,* edited by Michelle Szabo and Shelley Koch, 213–230. London: Bloomsbury.

Roos, G., R. Prättälä, and K. Koski. 2001. "Men, Masculinity and Food: Interviews with Finnish Carpenters and Engineers." *Appetite* 37: 47–56.

Rosenberg, Nathan and Clay East. 2018. "Sorry, Pretty Much Everyone: Young Farmers Are the Least Diverse—and Smallest—Group of Farmers in the Country." New Food Economy. Accessed March 27, 2018. https://newfoodeconomy.org/debunk-rise-young-farmer-myth.

Rosner, Helen. 2017. "Mario Batali and the Appetites of Men." *New Yorker.* Accessed January 2, 2018. https://www.newyorker.com/culture/annals-of-gastronomy/mario-batali-and-the-appetites-of-men.

Rousset S., P. Patureau Mirand, M. Brandolini, J. F. Martin, and Y. Boirie. 2003. "Daily Protein Intakes and Eating Patterns in Young and Elderly French." *British Journal of Nutrition* 90(6): 1107–1115.

Sachs, C., P. Allen, A. Terman, J. Hayden, and C. Hatcher. 2014. "Front and Back of the House: Socio-spatial Inequalities in Food Work." *Agriculture and Human Values* 31(1): 3–17.

Sachs, Carolyn. 1996. *Gendered Fields: Rural Women, Agriculture, and Environment.* Boulder, CO: Westview Press.

Sachs, Carolyn and Margaret Alston. 2010. "Global Shifts, Sedimentations, and Imaginaries: An Introduction to the Special Issue on Women and Agriculture." *Signs* 35(2): 277–287.

Sachs, Carolyn, Mary E. Barbercheck, Kathryn Brasier, Nancy Ellen Kiernan, and Anna Rachel Terman. 2016. *The Rise of Women Farmers and Sustainable Agriculture.* Iowa City: University of Iowa Press.

Saguy, A. and K. Gruys. 2010. "Morality and Health: News Media Constructions of Overweight and Eating Disorders." *Social Problems* 57(2): 231–250.

Saguy, Abigail C. 2013. *What's Wrong with Fat?* New York: Oxford University Press.

Sainsbury, Diane. 2004. "Women's Political Representation in Sweden: Discursive Politics and Institutional Presence." *Scandinavian Political Studies* 27(1): 65–87.

Sanchez, Teresa. 2015. "Gendered Sharecropping: Waged and Unwaged Mexican Immigrant Labor in the California Strawberry Fields." *Signs* 40(1): 917–938.

Sandberg, Erik. 2010. "The Retail Industry in Western Europe: Trends, Facts and Logistics Challenges." Linköping, Sweden: Linköping University Electronic Press.

Saugeres, Lise. 2002. "'She's Not Really a Woman, She's Half a Man': Gendered Discourses of Embodiment in a French Farming Community." *Women's Studies International Forum* 25(6): 641–650.

Sayer, L. C. 2005. "Gender, Time and Inequality: Trends in Women's and Men's Paid Work, Unpaid Work and Free Time." *Social Forces* 84(1): 285–303.

Schippers, Mimi. 2007. "Recovering the Feminine Other: Masculinity, Femininity, and Gender Hegemony." *Theory and Society* 36: 85–102.

Scrinis, G. 2013. *Nutritionism: The Science and Politics of Dietary Advice.* New York: Columbia University Press.

Sellaeg, Kari and Gwen Chapman. 2008. "Masculinity and Food Ideals of Men Who Live Alone." *Appetite* 51(1): 120–128.

Shannon, Jerry. 2014. "What Does SNAP Benefit Usage Tell Us About Food Access in Low-Income Neighborhoods?" *Social Science and Medicine* 107: 89–99.

Shierholz, Heidi. 2014. *Low Wages and Few Benefits Mean Many Restaurant Workers Can't Make Ends Meet.* Washington, DC: Economic Policy Institute, 2014.

Shiva, Vandana. 1993. "Reductionism and Regeneration: A Crisis in Science." In *Ecofeminism*, edited by Maria Mies and Vandana Shiva, 22–35. London: Zed Books.

Shortall, Sally. 1999. *Women and Farming: Property and Power.* London: Macmillan.

Siever, M. 1994. "Sexual Orientation and Gender as Factors in Socioculturally Acquired Vulnerability to Body Dissatisfaction and Eating Disorders." *Journal of Consulting and Clinical Psychology* 62: 252–260.

Slocum, Rachel. 2007. "Whiteness, Space and Alternative Food Practice." *Geoforum* 38(3): 520–533.

———. 2008. "Thinking Race Through Corporeal Feminist Theory: Divisions and Intimacies at the Minneapolis Farmer's Market." *Social & Cultural Geography* 9: 849–869.

Smith, Dorothy. 1987. *The Everyday World as Problematic*. Boston: Northeastern University Press.

———. 2005. *Institutional Ethnography: A Sociology for the People*. New York: Rowman & Littlefield.

Smith, L. P., S. W. Ng, and B. M. Popkin. 2013. "Trends in US Home Food Preparation and Consumption: Analysis of National Nutrition Surveys and Time Use Studies from 1965–1966 to 2007–2008." *Nutrition Journal* 12: 45.

Smith, Sharon. 1997. "Engels and the Origin of Women's Oppression." *International Socialist Review* 2.

Sobal, J., L. K. Kahn, and C. Bisogni. 1998. "A Conceptual Model of the Food and Nutrition System." *Social Science and Medicine* 47(7): 853–863.

Sobal, Jeffery. 2005. "Men, Meat and Marriage: Models of Masculinity." *Food and Foodways* 13(1): 135–158.

———. 2008. "Sociological Analysis of the Stigmatisation of Obesity." In *A Sociology of Food and Nutrition: The Social Appetite*, edited by John Germov and Lauren Williams, 381–400. 3rd ed. South Melbourne, Australia: Oxford University Press.

Som Castellano, Rebecca L. 2015. "Alternative Food Networks and Food Provisioning as a Gendered Act." *Agriculture and Human Values* 32(3): 461–474.

———. 2016. "Alternative Food Networks and the Labor of Food Provisioning: A Third Shift?" *Rural Sociology* 81(3): 445–469.

Sprague, Joey. 1988. "The Other Side of the Banner: Toward a Feminization of Politics." In *Seeing Female: Social Roles and Personal Lives*, edited by Sharon Brehm, 159–171. Westport, CT: Greenwood Press.

Statistics Canada. 2015. "Labour Force Characteristics by Sex and Age Group." Statistics Canada. Accessed March 12, 2015. http://www.statcan.gc.ca/tables-tableaux/sum-som/l01/cst01/labor05-eng.htm.

Stewart, Lockie. 2009. "Responsibility and Agency Within Alternative Food Networks: Assembling the 'Citizen Consumer.'" *Agriculture and Human Values* 26(3): 193–201.

Stibbe, A. 2012. "Advertising, Gender and Health Advice: The Case of Men's Health in the Year 2000." *Masculinities and Social Change* 1(3): 190–209. doi: 10.4471/MCS.2012.13.

Strings, Sabrina. 2015. "Obese Black Women as 'Social Dead Weight': Reinventing the 'Diseased Black Woman.'" *Signs: Journal of Women in Culture & Society* 41(1): 107–130.

Strong, S. M., D. A. Williamson, R. G. Netemeyer, and J. H. Geer. 2000. "Eating Disorder Symptoms and Concerns About Body Differ as a Function of Gender and Sexual Orientation." *Journal of Social and Clinical Psychology* 19: 240–255.

Sumner, Jennifer and Sophie Llewelyn. 2011. "Organic Solutions? Gender and Organic Farming in the Age of Industrial Agriculture." *Capitalism Nature Socialism* 22(1): 100–118. doi: 10.1080/10455752.2010.546659.

Swenson, Rebecca. 2009. "Domestic Divo? Televised Treatments of Masculinity, Femininity and Food." *Critical Studies in Media Communication* 26(1): 36–53.

Szabo, Michelle. 2013. "Foodwork or Foodplay? Men's Domestic Cooking, Privilege and Leisure." *Sociology* 47(4): 623–638.

———. 2014. "Men Nurturing Through Food: Challenging Gender Dichotomies Around Domestic Cooking." *Journal of Gender Studies* 23(1): 18–31.

Szabo, Michelle and Shelley Koch. 2017. "Introduction." In *Food, Masculinities and Home: Interdisciplinary Perspectives*, edited by Michelle Szabo and Shelley Koch, 1–28. London: Bloomsbury.

Szasz, Andrew. 2007. *Shopping Our Way to Safety*. St. Paul: University of Minnesota Press.

Tarasuk, V. S. and G. H. Beaton. 1999. "Household Food Insecurity and Hunger Among Families Using Food Banks." *Canadian Journal of Public Health* 90(2): 109–113.

Thompson, Becky. 1994. *A Hunger So Wide and So Deep*. Minneapolis: University of Minnesota Press.

Tolich, Martin and Celia Briar. 1999. "Just Checking It Out: Exploring the Significance of Informal Gender Divisions Amongst American Supermarket Employees." *Gender, Work and Organization* 6(3): 129–133.

Trauger, Amy. 2004. "'Because They Can Do the Work': Women Farmers and Sustainable Agriculture." *Gender, Place and Culture* 11(2): 289–307.

Trauger, Amy, Carolyn C. Sachs, Mary E. Barbercheck, Kathryn J. Brasier, Nancy Ellen Kiernan, and Jill Findeis. 2008. "Agricultural Education: Gender Identity and Knowledge Exchange." *Journal of Rural Studies* 24(4): 432–439.

Trauger, Amy, Carolyn E. Sachs, Mary E. Barbercheck, Kathryn J. Brasier, Nancy Ellen Kiernan, and Audrey Schwarztberg. 2010. "The Object of Extension': Agricultural Education and Authentic Farmers in Pennsylvania USA." *Sociologia Ruralis* 50(2): 85–102.

Tronto, Joan. 2002. "The Nanny Question in Feminism." *Hypatia* 17(2): 34–51.

Twigg, J. 1983. "Vegetarianism and the Meanings of Meat." In *The Sociology of Food and Eating*, edited by A. Murcott, 18–30. Aldershot, UK: Gower Publishing.

U.S. Bureau of the Census. 2009. "Annual Social and Economic Supplement." Washington, DC: Government Printing Office.

U.S. Department of Agriculture (USDA). 2014a. "2012 Census of Agriculture: Characteristics of All Farms and Farms with Organic Sales." USDA. Accessed November 9, 2016. https://www.agcensus.usda.gov/Publications/2012/Online_Resources/Special_Organics_Tabulation/organictab.pdf.

———. 2014b. "Farm Demographics U.S. Farmers by Gender, Age, Race, Ethnicity, and More." USDA. Accessed March 13, 2016. https://www.agcensus.usda.gov/Publications/2012/Online_Resources/Highlights/Farm_Demographics/Highlights_Farm_Demographics.pdf.

———. 2015. "Retail Trends." USDA, Economic Research Service. Accessed January 15, 2016. http://www.ers.usda.gov/topics/food-markets-prices/retailing-wholesaling/retail-trends.aspx.

———. 2016a. "Crop Production 2015 Summary." National Agricultural Statistics Service ISSN: 1057–7823.

———. 2016b. "Definitions of Food Security." USDA, Economic Reserch Service. Accessed May 18, 2015. https://www.ers.usda.gov/topics/food-nutrition-assistance/food-security-in-the-us/definitions-of-food-security.

———. 2016c. "Food Away from Home as Percentage of Food Expenditures." USDA, Economic Reserch Service. https://www.ers.usda.gov/data-products/food-expenditures/food-expenditures/#Food Expenditures.

———. 2017a. "Food spending as a share of income declines as income rises." USDA, Economic Research Service. Accessed October 7, 2018. https://www.ers.usda.gov/data-products/chart-gallery/gallery/chart-detail/?chartId=58372.

———. 2017b. "Food Dollar Application." USDA, Economic Research Service. Accessed August 2017. https://data.ers.usda.gov/reports.aspx?ID=17885.

———. 2018. "Corn and Other Feedgrains: Background." USDA, Economic Research Service. May 15. Accessed May 28, 2018. https://www.ers.usda.gov/topics/crops/corn/background.aspx.

———. N.d. "Discrimination Lawsuits." USDA. Accessed June 2015. https://www.nrcs.usda.gov/Internet/FSE_DOCUMENTS/nrcs141p2_015583.pdf.

Van Esterik, Penny. 1999. "Right to Food; Right to Feed; Right to Be Fed: The Intersection of Women's Rights and the Right to Food." *Agriculture and Human Values* 16: 225–232.

Van Rossum, C., H. P. Fransen, J. Verdaik-Kloostermam, E. J. Buurma-Rethans, and M. Ocke. 2011. *Dutch National Food Consumption Survey 2007–2010.* Bilthoven, Netherlands: National Institute for Public Health and Environment. Accessed November 2017. http://www.rivm.nl/bibliotheek/rapporten/350050006.pdf.

Vartanian, L. R., C. P. Herman, and J. Polivy. 2007. "Consumption Stereotypes and Impression Management: How You Are What You Eat." *Appetite* 48: 265–277.

Ver Ploeg, Michele, Lisa Mancino, Jessica E. Todd, Dawn Marie Clay, and Benjamin Scharadin. 2015. "Where Do Americans Usually Shop for Food and How Do They Travel to Get There? Initial Findings from the National Household Food Acquisition and Purchase Survey." Economic Information Bulletin 138. Washington, DC: USDA.

Vespa, Jonathan, Jamie M. Lewis, and Rose M. Kreider. 2013. "America's Families and Living Arrangements: 2012 Population Characteristics." U.S. Census Bureau. Accessed November 14, 2017. https://www.census.gov/prod/2013pubs/p20-570.pdf.

Wade, T. D., A. Keski-Rahkonen, and J. Hudson. 2011. "Epidemiology of Eating Disorders." In *Textbook in Psychiatric Epidemiology,* edited by M. Tsuang and M. Tohen, 343–360. 3rd ed. New York: Wiley.

Wade-Gales, G. 1997. "'Laying on Hands' Through Cooking: Black Women's Majesty and Mystery in Their Own Kitchens." In *Through the Kitchen Window: Women Explore the Intimate Meanings of Food and Cooking,* edited by A. V. Avakian, 95–103. Oxford, UK: Berg.

Warde, A. and K. Hetherington. 1994. "English Households and Routine Food Practices: A Research Note." *Sociological Review* 42(4): 758–778.

Wardrop, J. 2006. "Private Cooking, Public Eating: Women Street Vendors in South Durban." *Gender, Place and Culture* 13(6): 677–683.

Wells, Betty. 1998. "Creating a Public Space for Women in US Agriculture: Empowerment, Organization and Social Change." *Sociologia Ruralis* 38(3): 371–390.

West, Candace, and Don H. Zimmerman. 1987. "Doing Gender." *Gender and Society* 1(2): 125–151.

Whatmore, Sarah. 1991. *Farming Women: Gender, Work and Family Enterprise.* Basingstoke, UK: Macmillan.

White, Monica M. 2011. "Sisters of the Soil: Urban Gardening as Resistance in Detroit." *Race/Ethnicity: Multidisciplinary Global Contexts* 5(1): 13–28.

———. 2017. "'A Pig and a Garden': Fannie Lou Hamer and the Freedom Farms Co-operative." *Food and Foodways* 25(1): 20–39.

White, T. Kirk and Robert Hoppe. 2012. "Changing Farm Structure and the Distribution of Farm Payments and Federal Crop Insurance." Economic Information Bulletin 91. Economic Research Service. Accessed December 10, 2015. https://www.ers.usda.gov/webdocs/publications/44650/13729_eib91_1_.pdf?v=41055.

Williams, Lauren and John Germov. 2008. "Constructing the Female Body: Dieting, the Thin Ideal and Body Acceptance." In *A Sociology of Food and Nutrition: The Social Appetite*, edited by John Germov and Lauren Williams, 329–362. 3rd ed. South Melbourne, Australia: Oxford University Press.

———. 2017. "From 'The Misses Used to Cook' to 'Get the Recipe Book and Get Stuck into It': Reconstructing Masculinities in Older Men." In *Food, Masculinities and Home: Interdisciplinary Perspectives*, edited by Michelle Szabo and Shelley Koch, 108–125. London: Bloomsbury.

Williams-Forson, Psyche. 2006. *Building Houses Out of Chicken Legs: Black Women, Food, and Power*. Chapel Hill: University of North Carolina Press.

Williamson, I. and P. Hartley. 1998. "British Research into the Increased Vulnerability of Young Gay Men to Eating Disturbance and Body Dissatisfaction." *European Eating Disorders Review* 6: 160–170.

Wilson, Gilbert Livingstone, ed. 1917 [1987]. "Buffalo Bird Woman's Garden Recounted by Maxi'diwiac (Buffalo Bird Woman) of the Hidatsa Indian Tribe (ca. 1839–1932)." University of Pennsylvania. Accessed November 15, 2015. http://digital.library.upenn.edu/women/buffalo/garden/garden.html.

Wood, S. D. and J. Gilbert. 2000. "Returning African-American Farmers to the Land: Recent Trends and a Policy Rationale." *Review of Black Political Economy* 27(4): 43–64.

Wright-St Clair, Valerie, Clare Hocking, Wannipa Bunrayong, Soisuda Vittayakorn, and Phuonjai Rattakorn. 2005. "Older New Zealand Women Doing the Work of Christmas: A Recipe for Identity Formation." *Sociological Review* 53(20): 332–350.

Wrigley, Neil, Daniel Warm, Barrie Margetts, and Amanda Whelan. 2002. "Assessing the Impact of Improved Retail Access on Diet in a 'Food Desert': A Preliminary Report." *Urban Studies* 39(11): 2061–2082.

Yelland, Christine and Marika Tiggemann. 2003. "Muscularity and the Gay Ideal: Body Dissatisfaction and Disordered Eating in Homosexual Men." *Eating Behaviors* 4: 107–116.

Yen Liu, Yvonne and Dominique Apollon. 2011. "The Color of Food." Applied Research Center. Accessed February 27, 2015. https://www.raceforward.org/sites/default/files/downloads/food_justice_021611_F.pdf.

York, Richard and Shannon Bell. 2014. "Life Satisfaction Across Nations: The Effects of Women's Political Status and Public Priorities." *Social Science Research* 48: 48–61.

Zukin, Sharon. 2004. *Point of Purchase: How Shopping Changed American Culture*. New York: Routledge.

Index